SEMINAR SELLING

The Ultimate Resource Guide for Marketing Financial Services

Paul Karasik

IRWIN
Professional Publishing

Chicago • Bogotá • Boston • Buenos Aires • Caracas
London • Madrid • Mexico City • Sydney • Toronto

Editor-in-chief: Jeffrey A. Krames
Marketing manager: Tiffany Dykes
Project editor: Mary Conzachi
Production supervisor: Dina L. Treadaway
Designer: Jeanne Rivera
Manager, graphics and desktop services: Kim Meriwether
Compositor: Precision Graphics
Typeface: 11/14 Palatino
Printer: Maple-Vail Book Manufacturing Group

Library of Congress Cataloging-in-Publication Data

Karasik, Paul, 1947–
    Seminar selling : the ultimate resource guide for marketing
financial services / Paul Karasik.
        p.   cm.
    Includes index.
    ISBN 0-7863-0351-4
    1. Financial services industry—United States—Marketing.
2. Seminars—United States—Marketing.   I. Title.
HG181.K28   1995
332.1'068'8—dc20   94–37804

Printed in the United States of America

1 2 3 4 5 6 7 8 9 0 MV 1 0 9 8 7 6 5 4

This book is dedicated to all financial industry professionals who seek to master new and innovative ways to market their products and services more successfully. The quality of this book and my efforts can only be measured in your professional achievements.

Acknowledgments

My deepest appreciation to all of the financial planners, registered reps, insurance agents, attorneys, accountants, financial product wholesalers, and bank investment representatives who have generously shared their experiences and their insights on seminar selling with me.

And I am most grateful to all people who sell and share my enthusiasm and dedication to this fascinating art and science. I honor you and your personal efforts. Your success in sales and marketing is the noble and mighty power that drives the engine of all business.

Preface

When the opportunity to write this book presented itself, I became excited by the thought of creating a definitive resource on seminar selling in the financial services industry.

I've had more than 21 years experience as a professional salesperson. Sales has been in my blood my entire life. My father, his brothers, my mother, my sister, and most of my cousins have made a career in sales.

My first two books, *Sweet Persuasion* and *Sweet Persuasion for Managers* (Simon & Schuster), received wide acceptance and were very popular among financial industry professionals. These books introduced selling strategies based on service and genuine concern for the prospect, a method of selling that is critical to financial success.

I began delivering international personal growth programs in New York City, and it was there I was bitten by the seminar bug. I was attracted to the fun and excitement of group presentations, but more importantly, I found personal satisfaction sharing information with others.

After achieving financial success in sales, I began consulting organizations in the areas of sales, marketing, and management. I delivered sales training programs based upon the concept of building profitable client relationships to Fortune 500 companies. For the past seven years, I've been a professional seminar leader and management consultant for the financial industry. Since becoming a consultant, practically all of my efforts have been directed toward helping financial industry professionals market and sell their products.

How to Make It Big in the Seminar Business (McGraw-Hill), my first book on seminars, has become a bestseller in the business book division. "Seminar Selling," my monthly column published in *National Underwriter* magazine, is being used in a training text for a variety of financial organizations.

When I began working to solve sales and management problems for the financial industry, I immediately saw the benefits of group presentations. I became increasingly conscious of this incredible opportunity for financial planners, insurance agents, stockbrokers, and even banks. I also realized that this golden opportunity was not being taken advantage of. After analyzing this phenomenon, I have established two reasons why more individuals do not conduct financial seminars:

Reason #1: The individuals who are reaping the rewards of seminar selling are not anxious to share the information. There seems to be a veil of secrecy surrounding the seminar selling process. Many professionals refuse to share the tricks of the trade with their colleagues, especially those within the same organization.

Reason #2: Very little information is available. Even such fine resources as the International Association of Financial Planners and the National Association of Life Underwriters do not have information available on seminar selling.

Collecting and studying information on seminar selling became a fascination for me as a consultant. The process brought together the three most prominent elements in my professional career: selling, conducting seminars, and working with the financial industry. It has often been said that success comes more easily when you enjoy what you do. Consequently, I have achieved high status as one of the leading gurus in the seminar business.

Not long ago, I was asked to be the keynote speaker at the national conference of the International Association of Financial Planners of New Zealand. I watched in awe as people purchased copies of my book, *How to Make It Big in the Seminar Business*, faster than they could be taken out of their shipping boxes. It was then I realized the tremendous need in the financial industry for information on how to conduct seminars.

Seminar Selling addresses the issues that both established and aspiring seminar leaders need to know.

Today I am more enthusiastic than ever about the opportunities and benefits offered by this marketing strategy. There is no limit to seminar selling opportunities. The market for selling insurance, investment opportunities, and financial services of all kinds has barely been scratched. And there has never been a greater need for this book.

That's why I wrote it.

Paul Karasik

Contents

INTRODUCTION   1

What Is Seminar Selling? 1

Seminar Selling Is Not for Everyone, 1

Seminar Selling Is a Perfect Strategy for Attracting
  Qualified Prospects to You, 1

Seminar Selling Allows You to Leverage Your Time, 2

Seminar Selling Eliminates the Most Common
  Sales Objection, 3

Seminar Selling Is Perfect for the Mature
  Financial Marketplace, 4

Seminar Selling Is the Secret Success Strategy
  Everyone Knows, 4

Seminar Selling Is Fun, 5

How to Get the Most from This Book, 5

Part I
SEMINAR SELLING SUCCESS STRATEGIES
AND TECHNIQUES   7

Chapter One
SEMINAR SELLING: THE BIG PICTURE   9

Presentation Formats, 9
  Seminar, 9
  Speech, 10
  Workshop, 10

Promote Your Seminar as a Joint Venture, 10

Endless Opportunities: Public and In-House Seminars, 11
  Public Seminars, 11
  Sponsored or In-House Seminars, 12

Prerequisite for Your Success, 14
    Seminar Design Skills, 15
    Seminar Marketing Skills, 15
    Seminar Delivery Skills, 15
    Selling Skills, 16
Resources, 16

Chapter Two
THE PSYCHOLOGY OF SEMINAR SELLING   17

Understanding Your Objectives, 17
Focus on Your Psychological Advantages, 19
What Makes People Tick? 21
Don't Hesitate to Disturb People, 22

Chapter Three
TADA: THE CRITICAL SEMINAR
SELLING STRATEGY   23

TADA: The Foundation for a Winning
  Business Plan, 23
How to Choose a TADA, 24
    The Magic Wand Technique, 25
    The TADA Survey, 25
Suggested TADAs, 26

Chapter Four
HOW TO MASTER THE ART
OF CLOSING THE SALE   29

Initiate the Relationship During
  the Registration Process, 29
    Your Marketing Material, 29
    The Registration Contact, 30
    The Confirmation Letter, 32
    The Confirmation Phone Call, 22
Build Relationships at the Seminar, 22
    What to Do Before the Seminar Begins, 33

What to Do During the Seminar, 34

What to Do After the Seminar Ends, 34

WII-FM? 34

Two Invaluable Closing Techniques, 35

The Seminar Participant Evaluation, 36

The Ten Question Quiz, 0036

Closing at Your Complimentary Consultation, 38

Chapter Five
HOW TO DESIGN A PERFECT FINANCIAL SEMINAR

39

Assemble Your Mastermind Group, 39

Use Interviews to Focus Your Seminar, 40

The Modular Design Approach (MDA)
to Seminar Design, 41

How to Identify Your Seminar Modules, 41

Prioritize Your Modules, 43

Seven Ways to Make Your Content Rock Solid, 44

The Secret Ingredient to Your Seminar, 45

How to Get Approval by the National Association
of Securities Dealers, 46

Resources, 47

Chapter Six
SHOULD YOU BUY A PREPACKAGED SEMINAR OR MAKE YOUR OWN?

48

The Prepackaged Seminar, 48

Advantages of Prepackaged Seminars, 48

Disadvantages of Prepackaged Seminars, 49

Design Your Own Seminar, 50

The Combo Package, 51

Hire a Consultant, 51

Resources, 52

Chapter Seven
HOW TO CREATE IMPRESSIVE
HANDOUT MATERIALS   54

The Importance of Handouts, 54
What Your Handouts *Must* Include, 55
What Your Handouts Can Include, 55
How to Assemble Your Handouts, 57
   Three-Ring Binder, 57
   Bound Workbooks, 57
   Folder, 58
Resources, 58

Chapter Eight
HOW TO CHOOSE AND USE AUDIOVISUALS 61

Why You Should Use Visual Aids, 61
How to Choose the Best Visual Aid, 62
   Slide Projector, 62
   Overhead Projector, 63
   Flipchart and Marker Board, 63
Guidelines for Using All Visual Aids, 64
Resources, 65
The "Turn, Touch, Talk" Technique, 67
Putting the Audio into Your Audiovisuals, 67
The Four Styles of Microphones, 68
Guidelines for Using Microphones and Sound Systems, 69
Tape Recorders and CD Players for Using
  Prerecorded Sound, 70
Resources, 70
Final Advice on Audiovisual Equipment, 71

Chapter Nine
CHOOSING THE TIME AND PLACE
OF YOUR SEMINAR   72

Check Your Calendar, 72
Best Months and Days of the Week, 72
Choosing the Best Time of Day, 73

Provide an Alternate Choice, 73

Choosing the Best Seminar Site, 74

Resources, 75

How to Minimize Meeting Room Expenses, 76

The Meeting Room Confirmation Letter, 76

Chapter Ten
HOW TO PRODUCE WINNING
MARKETING MATERIAL   78

The Three Primary Formats, 78

Resources, 78

Focus on Your Target Audience, 79

How to Write Hot Copy, 79

Resources, 82

What to Include in Your Brochure
  or Marketing Material, 82
  Promotional Materials Checklist, 82

Resources, 85

The Three Most Successful Direct-Mail Approaches, 85
  The Brochure, 85
  The Letter Invitation, 88
  The Wedding Style Seminar Invitation, 89

Should You Use a Professional to Design
  Your Material? 90
  Graphic Designers, 91

Resources, 91
  Copywriters, 91

Resources, 92
  Advertising Agencies and Public Relations Firms, 92

How to Find the Best Printer, 92

Chapter Eleven
HOW TO PROMOTE YOUR SEMINAR
WITH DIRECT MAIL   94

Resources, 94

How to Choose the Right Mailing List, 95

Where to Purchase a Mailing List, 95

Mailing List Components, 96

How to Get the Best Mailing List, 97

How to Test Your Direct-Mail Program
  with the A/B Split Method, 98

Test Before You Invest, 99

Resources, 100

Cost of Direct-Mail Promotion, 100

Checklist and Timeline for Your Direct-Mail Program, 101

Chapter Twelve
**FILLING YOUR SEMINAR SEATS
WITH ADVERTISEMENTS**   102

Choosing the Best Advertising Medium, 102

Resources, 103

Nine Rules for Creating a Successful
  Newspaper Ad, 103

Resources, 106

Getting the Best Response from Your
  Newspaper Ad, 106

Is Radio or Television Advertising Appropriate
  for You? 107

Resources, 108

Chapter Thirteen
**INCREASING REGISTRATIONS
WITH FREE PUBLICITY**   109

Become Your Own Press Agent, 109

Eight Steps to Getting Media Coverage, 109

Resources, 110

Nine Components of a Professional Media Kit, 112

   1. Press Release, 112

   2. Cover Letter, 114

   3. Bio, 115

   4. Photograph, 116

Resources, 116

5. Tearsheets and List of Previous Appearances, 116

6. Articles and Books You've Written, 117

7. Seminar Brochure, 117

8. Company Brochure, 117

9. Sample Question List, 117

Resources, 118

A Guaranteed Method for Getting
on National Talk Shows, 118

How to Turn Publicity into Profits, 119

The "Mighty Mouse" Method for Free
Seminar Promotion, 119

Chapter Fourteen
USING THE TELEPHONE TO MARKET YOUR SEMINAR   121

Advantages and Disadvantages
of Telephone Marketing, 121

Hiring Your Callers, 122

Results You Can Expect, 123

The Script and How to Make It Work, 124

The Best Time to Make Calls, 126

Daily Tracking Sheets, 126

Following Up to Reduce No-Shows, 128

Creating a Telephone Seminar Marketing Machine, 128

Chapter Fifteen
THE "UNSEMINAR": AN ADVANCED SEMINAR SELLING STRATEGY   129

What Exactly Is an "Unseminar"? 129

The Prerequisite Is a Current Client List, 130

Why the Unseminar Format Works, 130

Promoting the Unseminar Is Relatively Inexpensive, 131

Conducting Your Program Is Simple and Relaxed, 132

Some Important Guidelines for Achieving
Optimum Profitability, 132

Receive Immediate and Long-Term Rewards, 133

Chapter Sixteen
HOW TO TAP THE CORPORATE MARKET WITH SEMINAR SELLING   135

TADA: The Magic Marketing Strategy, 135
The Winning Strategy PMP: Phone–Mail–Phone, 136
Presenting Your Material, 139
   Cover Letter, 139
   Seminar Brochure and Company Brochure, 140
   Client List and Endorsements, 140
   Seminar Materials, 141
Phone to Follow-up, 141
Organize Your Leads, 143
Resources, 143
For Free or Fee?, 144

Chapter Seventeen
HOW TO CAPITALIZE ON THE IN-HOUSE SEMINAR MARKET   145

Get Paid to Sell Your Services, 145
Trade and Professional Associations, 147
Resources, 147
Adult and Continuing Education Organizations, 148
Service Clubs and Fraternal Organizations, 148
Church and Religious Organizations, 149
Marketing Strategies for In-House Seminars, 149
How to Get Booked by Speakers Bureaus, 150

Chapter Eighteen
ARRANGING YOUR SEMINAR ROOM FOR SUCCESS   151

Seminar Room Temperature, 151
Seminar Room Lighting, 152
Seminar Room Seating, 152
Registration Table, 160

Chapter Nineteen
THE SECRETS OF THE WORLD'S
GREATEST SEMINAR LEADERS   161

The Essential Elements of Personal
  Presentation Skills, 161
What Is the Best Presentation Style? 164
Your Primary Objective as a Presenter, 165
Mastering the Art of "Educainment", 165
Resources, 167
How to Handle Q and A Like a Pro, 168
How to Get Really Good, 168

Chapter Twenty
GETTING YOUR BUTTERFLIES
TO FLY IN FORMATION   171

Nine Steps to Conquering Nervousness, 171
How to Deal With Difficult Seminar Participants, 175

Part Two
RESOURCE DIRECTORY   181

Financial Industry Publications, 183
Banking, Finance, and Insurance Associations, 191
Speakers Bureaus and Cruise Line Bureaus, 200
National Seminar Sites for Financial Seminars, 216

INDEX   232

Introduction

WHAT IS SEMINAR SELLING?

Seminar selling is an elegant and efficient way to sell and market your products and services. It is a method of selling where there is practically no tension between you and the prospect.

The steps are simple. Conduct a seminar where you will offer solutions to a financial problem. Provide this seminar for free or for a nominal amount of money. At the conclusion of the seminar, offer participants the opportunity to speak with you personally about their specific problems. Assuming you can provide the services they need, you will earn the right to have these individuals as your customers or clients. It's that simple.

SEMINAR SELLING IS NOT FOR EVERYONE

Seminar selling is for financial industry professionals who are ready to establish and expand their client base as quickly as possible. If you want to attract motivated clients, increase sales, and make more money, this book is for you!

In many ways, selling financial services is no different than selling any other product or service. And contrary to the constant barrage of so-called new selling techniques, the actual selling process hasn't changed much since Eve convinced Adam of the benefits of eating the delicious apple. Yet the rise in marketing and operating costs, a higher level of competition, the overuse of current marketing techniques, and the lack of significant differences in financial products and services have all resulted in the need to rethink the selling process.

In addition, there are three classic problems that continually plague financial industry professionals who want to expand their client base. First, a steady supply of qualified prospects is needed. Second, time and energy must be leveraged. Third, trust and confidence must be established quickly, or profitable relationships cannot be created.

Winners in the financial services industry all have one thing in common: they all possess a successful and cost-effective marketing system. Seminar selling is one of the easiest and most powerful systems to implement; it solves the classic sales and marketing problems.

SEMINAR SELLING IS A PERFECT STRATEGY FOR ATTRACTING QUALIFIED PROSPECTS TO YOU

The person who attends your seminar has expressed a need. This prospect has a problem and is actively seeking a solution—a solution you can provide. This puts you miles ahead of tedious and time-consuming techniques such as cold calling. If you first have to convince prospects that they have a problem, you are creating twice as much work for yourself. You are also going to be half as successful.

Seminar selling allows you to increase your closing ratio substantially because your prospects are actively seeking solutions that you can provide.

SEMINAR SELLING ALLOWS YOU TO LEVERAGE YOUR TIME

Sales is a numbers game. The more people you speak to, the more sales you make. Why speak to one prospect when you can speak to 100 in the same amount of time? Seminars help you play the selling game and master the mathematics of sales.

Today more than ever, there is a need to make every minute count. It is far too risky to attend a luncheon or networking situation and hope you will have the opportunity to pick up a new client. Seminar selling leverages your time in the most efficient way.

SEMINAR SELLING ELIMINATES THE MOST COMMON SALES OBJECTION

Today's financial marketplace is highly competitive. Because financial products and services have become so similar, there are no longer easily definable differences. The difference is *you*.

Contrary to what seems to be the trend in new communication systems and information dispersion, sales has not become high-tech. Rather, sales has become a game of "high-touch." Prospects now make purchasing decisions based upon *who* is selling the services. Sales has become a game of establishing relationships. If you can master the art of creating positive relationships, you will prosper.

The most common—and probably the only—real sales objection is, "I don't trust you." Seminar selling provides the opportunity for you to meet with your prospect face-to-face and establish the trust that will be the foundation for your mutually rewarding relationship.

Most people understand your objectives for presenting a financial seminar and attend it for exactly those reasons. The seminar is the perfect setting for them to evaluate you. Seminars function similarly to the tasting process in an ice cream store that features 101 flavors. You walk in and say, "What's chocolate strawberry swirl like?" They pull out a tiny plastic spoon, fill it with that flavor, and suggest you try for yourself. If you like it, you buy it; if not, you try something else.

Seminar selling allows the prospect to get a taste of you without making any real commitment. (It would certainly be nice to have this same luxury when it comes to choosing all of our professional relationships.) Your job, of course, will be to present yourself in the most favorable light.

SEMINAR SELLING IS PERFECT FOR THE MATURE FINANCIAL MARKETPLACE

Because there has been a proliferation of telemarketing and direct mail in the financial sales industry in recent years, the prospective market has grown irritated and these methods have become ineffective. Nearly everyone has received at least one telephone call from someone selling stocks, bonds, or another type of financial product. Most people react by getting off the phone the moment they realize the nature of the call. Similarly, the direct mail marketing material enclosed with your monthly bank statement only confuses further anyone seriously seeking answers to their financial problems.

Seminars offer a fresh approach to marketing. Regardless of how many programs are presented, they will each remain unique and effective. It is very unlikely that the seminar selling approach will ever become overused.

SEMINAR SELLING IS THE SECRET SUCCESS STRATEGY EVERYONE KNOWS

Open up any local newspaper and most likely you will find an advertisement for an investment or tax reduction seminar. Tune in your radio to your favorite business talk show and you are very likely to hear an announcement for an upcoming financial seminar.

Interview any insurance agent or securities broker and ask this person who they know is using the seminar selling strategy. Undoubtedly they will know people who are using seminar selling and it will probably be the top producers in the office or region.

Ask the lay person if they are familiar with financial seminars and again you will probably get an affirmative answer. It quickly becomes apparent that financial seminars are extremely popular.

The Business Institute interviewed 67 financial industry professionals, as well as regional and district managers. The results of this research showed that 52 or 78% of the most successful individuals use some form of seminar selling or group presentation strategy.

The question becomes, "Why don't more people use seminar selling?" The answer is very simple. Seminar selling is not for everyone.

And why not? First, you must be willing to invest the time to learn the fundamentals of seminar selling, which many people are unable to do. Second, you must be willing to overcome any fears you might have about public speaking, also a difficult task for many. Third, you must understand the benefits of seminar selling and the advantages of having an effective marketing system.

Finally, you've got to really want to be a success. You've got to be hungry for the rewards you will reap by using the seminar selling method. If you have financial products and services you believe in and are willing to apply the strategies and techniques contained in this book, you are guaranteed to be a success.

SEMINAR SELLING IS FUN

Even successful professionals can become complacent. Seminar selling is a little bit of show business and for many sales people is a great way to stand in the spotlight. Seminar selling is always exciting and fun. It is practically impossible to not get somewhat exhilarated by the opportunity to deliver a presentation.

HOW TO GET THE MOST FROM THIS BOOK

This book is designed to be both a training and reference book. It does not take an academic approach to a problem; rather, it provides real life answers. This book is your road map to success.

If you are planning to begin presenting financial seminars, this book is for you. It will teach you the actual steps you need to take to achieve your goals, and it will show you how to avoid making costly errors that can dissuade you from continuing with your programs.

If you are currently presenting seminars but are not reaping the rewards you know you have earned, this book will teach you how to modify your program to create the profits you are looking for. When you implement the techniques in this book, you will impact your bottom line exponentially.

And, most importantly, you will learn the underlying strategies that will allow you to continue to develop and hone your personal seminar selling programs for a lifetime.

This book also provides valuable seminar business contacts who will support your seminar selling program in a variety of ways. These contacts will save you time, money, and effort. As my mother used to say, "It's not what you know, it's who you know!"

If you want to get the most from this book, refer to it often. Don't read it once. Read it periodically. It contains information you may not be ready for today but will definitely need tomorrow.

If you use this book correctly, you will succeed in making money through seminar selling. Then I will have accomplished *my* goal.

P A R T

I

SEMINAR SELLING SUCCESS STRATEGIES AND TECHNIQUES

Chapter One

Seminar Selling: The Big Picture

In order to take advantage of the benefits of seminar selling, it is important that you become familiar with the variety of formats and opportunities available. You must also establish a professional development strategy, which will enable you to guarantee your success with seminar selling.

PRESENTATION FORMATS

There are three basic presentation formats for delivering your presentation. All three formats offer equal potential for developing new business.

Seminar

A *seminar* is an exchange of information concerning one specific topic, and it is relatively short in duration (usually one to six hours in length). It is an adult learning experience that is designed to provide answers to specific problems.

The most critical component of this definition is that *the seminar is designed to solve problems.* Adults, as a rule, are not in a learning mode; they are interested in information that is relevant to solving their problems. Therefore, it is always important to focus on the relevance of the information you are presenting. By focusing on the problem-solving aspect of your program, you will eliminate the pressure that is created when you are in a selling mode.

Speech

The *speech* has many of the same components as a seminar, but it is usually an hour or less in length and is usually minimally interactive. A speech is usually a part of a larger program or event. For maximum effectiveness, a speech should always be viewed as a short seminar. The guidelines for presenting a financial seminar should be followed when delivering a speech.

Contacts: See the Seminar Leaders Resource Directory in this book under "Speakers Bureaus." Many of the speakers bureaus listed here are continually seeking qualified experts to speak on a variety of topics. You will not only receive the opportunity to speak before a group of potential clients, the speakers bureaus will pay you a fee.

Workshop

The *workshop* allows your prospects to participate in the seminar. It implies learning by doing. For example, during a workshop in a basic investment seminar, participants might actually use a calculator to figure out tax savings.

Referring to your program as a workshop can be an good strategy. The participants will feel they are more likely to have valuable experience.

For the sake of simplicity, speeches and workshops will be included in this book whenever seminars are referred to.

PROMOTE YOUR SEMINAR AS A JOINT VENTURE

There are a variety of synergistic and profitable seminar alliances you can establish. Based upon a win-win strategy, a joint seminar enables you to support each others' objectives. One of the best features about this approach is that you will reduce expenses and increase return on investment. The following are some ideal prospects for joint venture seminars:

1. Small banks. Many banks are now marketing in a more aggressive manner. They are interested in expanding their

services to existing clients and capturing new business. Offer a educational seminar to the bank and work out the details so that there are no conflicts. They may even pick up the promotion expenses. It will add credibility to you and open new markets for your services.

2. Accounting firms. Accounting firms are perfect partners to promote seminars on tax planning. They will share the cost of promotion and help to fill the seminar seats by offering their existing clients the opportunities to attend the seminar.

3. Attorneys. Topics such as estate planning often require an attorney to discuss the legal aspects of the process. When you hold a joint seminar, the attorney will acquire new clients and so will you. Each of you will add credibility to each other. Here again, you can share the promotion costs.

4. Product wholesalers. Call product wholesalers and let them know about your plans to conduct seminars. Ask them if they would like to sponsor the event. If you can present a credible plan and demonstrate the profitability of your seminar, you will have little trouble finding wholesalers who would like to become your partners. For the wholesaler, the seminar is a cost-effective strategy for getting in front of the right people.

ENDLESS OPPORTUNITIES: PUBLIC AND IN-HOUSE SEMINARS

There are two different types of seminars: public and in-house. Each has its advantages and both offer endless opportunities.

Public Seminars

Public seminars are what most people think of when the word seminar is mentioned. They are usually held in a hotel meeting room or similar public space. Although some public seminars can be major events attracting hundreds or even thousands of people, most public financial seminars attract about 50 people.

Public seminars are promoted through advertising or direct mail, and each participant registers separately. The seminar participants usually share a common financial problem or concern, but are otherwise not related.

The advantages of public seminars include the following:

1. Promotion is relatively simple. Direct-mail lists for a geographic area are reasonable to purchase, easy to obtain, and work quite well. Advertising in print and broadcast, while more expensive, fills a room quite easily.

2. Your audience has qualified itself. You can be sure everyone who has taken the time to attend your seminar has more than a passing interest in your financial topic. In fact, chances are they've got a major concern or problem they would like to attend to.

3. You control everything. It's your party, so you call the shots. All decisions that will result in your success are made by you.

4. Follow-up is easier. You can develop and implement your own system that will enable you to follow up with your prospects efficiently.

The disadvantages of public seminars include the following:

1. Certain markets are not likely to attend public seminars. While you may do fine presenting an estate-planning seminar to retired individuals, a target market of doctors or dentists will be more difficult to attract to your seminar.

2. Your ability to customize a seminar is limited. Because of the diversity of your participants, it is impossible to address a lot of specific issues. But if your program is for employees of a corporation, you can include specific information that will benefit that particular group.

3. Public seminars take a lot of work to put together. There are countless details involved in promoting and conducting public seminars. You will almost always find it necessary to employ assistance when planning a public seminar.

Sponsored or In-House Seminars

Sponsored or *in-house* seminars are sponsored by many types of organizations. The content of the in-house seminar is modified to address the specific needs of the group being addressed. The style of presentation can also be modified to make it more effective. Although in-house seminars are usually promoted by the organization, you must identify the decision makers within the organization and then market your seminar to those individuals.

There are a variety of in-house opportunities, such as the following:

1. Corporations. Corporations are interested in helping their employees secure a financial future. Topics presented at financial seminars within a corporation include: classic money management seminars, preretirement seminars, and group benefit seminars.

The need for in-house financial seminars at corporations is growing. In some cases, financial planners are asked to present to numerous branches of the corporation, after presenting a seminar at the first one.

2. Professional and trade associations. One of the primary functions of professional and trade associations is education. Consequently, these associations hold hundreds or thousands of meetings each year.

Your financial seminar can be a valuable asset to the programming of an association. If you can help them solve their problems, they will be more than happy to give you the opportunity to speak.

3. Adult and continuing education. Many colleges, universities, high schools, and even libraries offer noncredit courses for adults. Contact these institutions for information on offering financial seminars.

4. Nonprofit organizations often sponsor seminars for their membership. These organizations welcome programs that will help their members.

5. Service clubs. There are a variety of service clubs, such as the Lions, Rotary, and Kiwanis, that bring in speakers. Most of these clubs have regular monthly meetings and need a constant supply of fresh topics and presenters.

6. Religious organizations. Practically every church and religious organization offers a form of nonreligious adult education programming.

Like public seminars, there are advantages and disadvantages of in-house seminars. The advantages include the following:

1. Promoting your seminar is less complicated. Instead of having to plan and promote completely on your own, you need only market it to one or two decision makers. The organization provides the room and the people.

2. By definition, your group will be targeted. You will be speaking to a room filled with individuals who are specifically qualified for your products or services.

3. You will have very little administrative work. The sponsoring group will handle all of the various details of the meeting.

4. Your promotion costs will be minimum. Promotion can be very expensive, but a media kit is all that is required for in-house seminar selling. In some instances, organizations will even pay you an honorarium.

The following are some disadvantages of in-house seminars:

1. The sponsor can dictate the content of your seminar. You will have to follow the rules and guidelines established by the sponsor. Although you might not find this a major problem, it could affect your closing ratio.

2. The logistics might be less than favorable. The setting may not be ideal for your seminar, and that can compromise your effectiveness.

3. In-house seminars often take longer to book. A public seminar takes about six weeks to promote, but it might take six months to secure the opportunity to present your program at a corporation.

PREREQUISITE FOR YOUR SUCCESS

As a financial industry professional, you already possess the proper administrative and business skills. You also possess extensive expertise in the financial services industry. In fact, there is a good chance you are considered an expert on a specific financial topic. You might hold a professional designation such as CFP or CLU. That is as it should be, but that's not enough. To maximize your results in seminar selling, you will also need to develop expertise as a seminar leader.

The following describes the specific skills you will need to develop to become a successful seminar leader.

Seminar Design Skills

You don't need a PhD to create an effective presentation, but you do need to understand the elements that must be included when presenting a professional program.

Seminars must have a beginning, a middle, and an end. Each one of these elements must be thought out and integrated so that the participants feel as though they have received what they came for.

Whether you are delivering a prepackaged seminar that you have purchased or a seminar your organization designed, you will need to know how to customize this program to accomplish your goals. You will continually have to modify your seminar to fit a variety of time frames, logistical challenges, and audience needs. When you understand these few basic seminar design techniques, you will possess the flexibility you need as a successful seminar leader.

Seminar Marketing Skills

You may have a great seminar, but you need people in the room if you want to make money. The primary tools for marketing remain the same: telephone, direct mail, and advertising. There are specific techniques used to adapt these tools for seminar selling.

If you plan presenting a public or in-house seminar, you will need to learn marketing skills that will fill your seats with high-quality participants.

Seminar Delivery Skills

The single most important skill you will need is the ability to deliver a great seminar. Many people consider themselves great speakers. That's a good start, but there are specific techniques you will need to master if you expect to control a seminar audience. A good seminar leader can facilitate activities and motivate and connect with an audience.

Selling Skills

Although seminar selling has softened your approach and established a buying environment, you will need to vary your selling skills at almost every point in the seminar selling process. First, you will need to sell the benefits of attending your seminar to people who inquire about it. You will also need to sell these benefits to decision makers at various organizations. But most importantly, you will need to sell yourself at the seminar and later at the business appointments you will be setting up.

The seminar selling process allows you to market your financial services without any kind of hard sell approach. As a matter of fact, in many cases prospects will be asking you to take care of their needs. Always keep in mind that you are creating an optimum buying environment when you use the seminar forum.

RESOURCES

The only organization that offers professional development for seminar leaders is the American Seminar Leaders Association. ASLA teaches individuals how to design, market, and deliver seminars. It holds an annual conference, training programs, and a "Seminar Leaders University." It also offers newsletters, books, tapes, educational programs, and a seminar-leaders certification program.

American Seminar Leaders Association
206 Sacramento St., Suite 201
Nevada City, CA 95959
(800) 735-0511 or (916) 265-2685
Fax (916) 265-2338

Chapter Two

The Psychology of Seminar Selling

UNDERSTANDING YOUR OBJECTIVES

Obviously, your number one purpose for conducting financial seminars is to sell financial products and services. Yet, many financial industry professionals lack a clear understanding of their specific objectives. Without a firm grasp of those objectives, you will never culminate into closing sales. Let's begin by discussing a few misconceptions of seminar selling:

1. **Financial seminars do not provide a thorough education.** No one attending a financial seminar is naive enough to believe he or she will become fully knowledgeable on a financial topic after attending a seminar for just several hours. Some topics, such as estate planning, will even require additional experts such as lawyers or accountants. But you will certainly be able to lay down the *fundamentals* of the topic. You will also provide a lot of valuable information including tips, strategies, and techniques.

Avoid setting yourself up for failure. You will disappoint yourself and your participants if you even imply they will learn everything they need to know about a particular financial issue.

Financial Seminar Success Principle #1

Always deliver more information than you promise and never promise more than you will deliver.

Keep yourself focused on the benefits of attending the seminar. Remember, the primary reason people attend seminars is to solve their problems, not to learn. Learning anything else is merely a feature. Most people would rather have their problem solved than to learn about how to solve them themselves.

2. **Financial seminars are not opportunities for you to display your oratory skills.** There's nothing wrong with having confidence or well-developed public speaking skills. But if you if you get too absorbed in the performance rather than the presentation, your investment of time, energy, and money will be wasted—and so will that of your audience.

Financial Seminar Success Principle #2

Stay focused on the elegance of your financial products and services rather than the eloquence of your own voice.

---

3. **Financial seminars are not for hard selling.** People do not like to be sold. They like to buy.

Each day, the average individual is bombarded with literally hundreds of sales messages. Even salespeople get overwhelmed by the constant barrage of advertisements and direct sales messages.

There's an old joke. If you want to be left alone on an airplane, tell the person next to you that you are an insurance salesperson. Although there is some humor in the joke, there is also a lot of truth.

The biggest mistake many seminar leaders make is using the hard-sell approach. Despite the incredible integrity and professionalism of most salespeople in the world, selling in not viewed as a noble profession.

One of the primary reasons people enjoy attending financial seminars is that they do not want to be sold. As soon as you (consciously or unconsciously) go into a selling mode, you will turn your audience off.

Financial Seminar Success Principle #3

Create an environment that motivates your audience to buy.

FOCUS ON YOUR PSYCHOLOGICAL ADVANTAGES

The real power of seminar selling lies in a few subtle elements of the seminar-selling format itself. By being aware of the power of the process, you will maximize your effectiveness.

The seminar format transforms your *position*. You are no longer just a planner, accountant, stock broker, or insurance broker. As a seminar leader, you are perceived in several different roles:

1. Teacher. We discussed the fact that a financial seminar does not provide participants with a thorough education on a topic, but it does put you in the position of teacher, or guru, and those who attend become your students. Even though this is a self-created position, it gives you a substantial amount of power.

Teachers are not always loved, but they almost always respected. The respect you will receive as a seminar leader will be amplified by your personal commitment to the position. Respect is one of the underlying tenets in most successful business relationships.

2. Counselor. According to Webster, a counselor is someone who gives advice. It is easy for you to make the transition from being someone standing in the front of a room giving advice to someone sitting in a one-to-one situation providing specific personal financial direction.

3. Problem solver. Your goal as a seminar leader is not to solve problems, but to prove to prospects that you *can* solve problems. Although many people don't like problem solvers, they all need them. If people attending your seminar are convinced you will provide them with solutions, profitable relationships will be created.

4. Friend. Yes, you are in a position to be a friend people can share their troubles with. You are in a position to learn about an intimate part of people's lives: their finances.

The psychological advantages of positioning yourself as a teacher, counselor, problem solver, and friend allows you a more personable and comfortable position than normally encountered in a selling situation.

The financial seminar is a kind of first date. The person attending your seminar will be consciously and probably subconsciously making the decision of whether or not to continue "seeing" you and being your friend.

It is very difficult to provide valid answers to financial problems without looking at the big picture. You must understand their needs based on who they are, what their specific personal needs are, what their current position is, and where they would like to be in the future.

It is important for financial industry professionals to understand and use these unique advantages when conducting a seminar. Remember, you are doing more than just selling a room full of people your products and services. You are selling yourself.

The Seminar Selling Golden Rule

The purpose of the financial seminar is to *initiate* multiple, mutually profitable, long term relationships.

Even the finest financial products and services are worthless without customers. One-time customers are good, but long-term client relationships are by far the most valuable assets to a successful business. Focus your energy on initiating solid, long-term relationships.

By understanding the psychological aspects of seminar selling, your efforts will be built on a stone foundation. Approaching the financial seminar with the correct mind-set is the key to achieving success and maximizing returns from your financial seminars.

WHAT MAKES PEOPLE TICK?

Although your head might be filled with wonderful thoughts and lots of good intentions as you present your seminar, you will need to understand and focus the content, comments, and delivery on the radio station everyone at the seminar is listening to: WII-FM? That's, "What's in it for me?"

For the most part, people spend most of their waking hours each day thinking about themselves. The people who attend your seminar aren't interested in just the information itself; they are interested in how that information will impact their lives. Therefore, it is your job to continually remind the participants in your seminar how your information affects *them*. For instance, "Let me show you how you can reduce *your* taxes by up to 25 percent this year." Or, "How does it feel knowing *your* grandchildren might only receive 20 percent of your estate, while Uncle Sam takes the rest? Let me show you how to avoid this problem."

Although it seems obvious to you, don't assume your participants have the capacity to connect your information with how it works.

The Law of Motivation

All human behavior stems from two basic desires: to gain rewards or avoid punishment.

If you want to speak the language of the people who attend your seminar, focus on the benefits. Many financial industry professionals fall into the trap of getting lost in numbers. Very few people who attend a financial seminar will ever be able to understand all the mathematics as well as you do, nor do they care to. People understand the effects of profit and loss, and that's what they want to hear about.

While this can be challenging, it is not an impossible task. It is a basic strategy that must permeate your marketing materials, your preseminar contact, your seminar script, your one-on-one interviews, and any follow-up you do.

Remember, your participant is continually asking the question, "What's in it for me?" Your job is to continually answer that question.

DON'T HESITATE TO DISTURB PEOPLE

There is a crisis in America. Most Americans fail to realize the importance of proper financial planning and the need to take control of their finances. It is your responsibility to convey a message that will inspire fear in the hearts and minds of the people who attend your seminar. Your mission is to disturb people enough for them to take action.

Nonaction is a form of action. You must emphasize that failure to take action will produce negative results. As a presenter you must be passionate about helping them to avoid the problems that will result from procrastination.

The Ultimate Law of Motivation

Pain and discomfort are the touchstones for action.

Chapter Three

TADA: The Critical Seminar Selling Strategy

Your seminar selling program will be successful if you build your business plan on two essential strategies: TADA and WII-FM.

TADA: THE FOUNDATION FOR A WINNING BUSINESS PLAN

Target Audience Design Approach (TADA) is your blueprint for seminar success. When planning a seminar, you will be faced with a myriad of decisions. The Target Audience Design Approach will provide you with a guideline for making the best decisions every time.

For example, let's assume your target audience is doctors. It is very unlikely that doctors would be willing to attend a weekday seminar. Using TADA, the best day would be Saturday. However, if you are planning an estate planning seminar for retired people, a weekday afternoon would be the best.

Similarly, if you want to conduct seminars for accountants, you would want to avoid any week in the months before April 15. If your TADA is for retail shops owners, the holiday season would be a poor choice, while February or March would be preferable.

The Target Audience Design Approach will guide you in making decisions about such elements as the following:

- The layout and copy of your marketing materials.
- Where you choose to advertise.

- The best seminar site.
- The length of your program.
- The type of seminar—public or in-house.
- The best mailing list.
- The best day, month, and time.

You might currently be somewhat of a generalist. Perhaps you sell mutual funds, insurance, or financial planning services to anyone who asks. You might even be doing well with this approach. But to be able to be successful at seminar selling, you will need to use TADA.

We live in an age of specialists. Just ask yourself, Who earns more money, a general practitioner or a cardiovascular surgeon? Likewise, you need to identify which target market you'd be most successful with and then use TADA to capture it.

HOW TO CHOOSE A TADA

There are two methods for choosing a TADA, depending on your level of experience and whether or not you have an existing client base.

For the individual who is experienced or who is working with an organization with an existing client list, the process is more of an identification process. Your objective is to analyze the characteristics of your clients and determine the most common elements. Who is your real market?

This analysis should, of course, include profitability. You may have 50 clients who fit a particular description, but if they only account for a small portion of your business, you must consider that when determining if a targeted seminar would be profitable. You may also have some subjective decisions to make, such as which products or services you would prefer to sell.

The newcomer to seminar selling is faced with the much greater challenge of actually *creating* a TADA, where it is a matter of choosing rather than identifying. In either case, the following are a few exercises that can help you with your TADA.

The Magic Wand Technique

The "Magic Wand Technique" is great for determining your TADA. Answer the following question to see how it works:

> If I had a magic wand and could make the ideal client appear for you, what would this person look like? Describe in detail.

The TADA Survey

Use this survey to help you focus on your exact TADA. Here is a list of elements to consider when you choose your TADA.

The TADA Survey Form

Answer as many of these questions as you can. Then summarize your answers.

1. Who needs my particular products and services?

2. What type of person do I feel most comfortable with?

3. What age group do I connect with best?

4. Where is my ideal prospect most likely to live? Be specific.

5. How is my ideal prospect employed?

6. What kind of educational background does this individual have?

7. What is the income level of my ideal prospect?

8. To what organizations does my ideal prospect belong?

9. Where does my ideal prospect go for financial information?

Don't waste your money attracting unqualified prospects. Don't waste your money advertising in the wrong places. Don't waste your time conducting seminars for the wrong audience. Begin with a TADA!

SUGGESTED TADAs

The following are some examples of TADAs that are very focused. Any one of these are excellent choices. The only incorrect choice is no choice.

1. Age.

   Heads of households between 25 and 39 years of age who are planning for the future.

   Heads of households between the ages of 40 and 49 who are seeking investment strategies with tax advantages.

   Heads of households between the ages of 50 and 59 who have disposable dollars and substantial reserves in CDs and retirement plans.

   Senior citizens between the ages of 65 and 79 years of age who have a significant amount of assets.

2. Geographical areas.

   New residents in the area.

   Heads of households within a designated area who have resided there for a significant amount of time.

3. Income level.

   Heads of household who earn $35,000+ per year.

   Heads of households who earn $50,000+ per year.

   Heads of households who earn $75,000+ per year.

   Heads of households who earn $100,000+ per year.

4. Occupation.

   Accountants.

   Athletes.

   Attorneys.

CPAs.

Dentists.

Engineers.

Opticians.

Optometrists.

Osteopaths.

Veterinarians.

Pharmacists.

Physicians.

Podiatrists.

Teachers.

5. Business owners.

Owners of businesses with 1–10 employees.

Owners of businesses with 2–20 employees.

Owners of businesses with 20+ employees.

6. Corporate position.

Sales managers.

Vice presidents.

Chief financial officers.

Department heads.

Purchasing agents.

7. Gender.

Men only.

Women only.

Divorced men or women.

Widowed men or women.

8. Financial specialty.

Health benefit plans.

401(k) plans.

Life insurance.

Disability insurance.

Preretirement planning.

Charitable giving.

Living trusts.

Financial planning for corporate employees.

Mutual funds.

Bonds.

Tax-advantaged investments.

College planning.

By using TADA you will avoid making costly marketing mistakes. Although it appears you are limiting your market, just the opposite is true. You will be establishing yourself as an expert and becoming a big fish in a small pond.

Remember TADA will put you on the fast track to success. Practically every instance of success in seminar selling can be traced to TADA, which is your passport to success.

Chapter Four

How to Master the Art of Closing the Sale

Strong business relationships are where the money is. Focus on building a relationship with your prospect and you will close the sale. Lose sight of this objective, and you will lose the sale. Let's take a look at the techniques you must use to build the relationships between you and your seminar participants.

INITIATE THE RELATIONSHIP DURING THE REGISTRATION PROCESS

You have four primary opportunities to initiate the relationship during the registration process: via your marketing material, the registration contact, the confirmation letter, and the confirmation phone call. The value of each of these potential relationship-building elements is described briefly below.

Your Marketing Material

Have you ever looked at an advertisement for a new movie in the newspaper and made a decision about wanting to see it? Have you ever received a piece of direct mail and made a decision about responding to it based upon how it looked and how it made you feel? These same not so subtle forms of communication are attracting your prospects to you or are pushing them away. Your prospect will be making decisions about you based in part upon your marketing effort. Be sure to evaluate your material by asking, "Would my target audience want to get to know me based upon my marketing material?"

It is important that your marketing material has a TADA and that it answers WII-FM. You can do this with the words you use and with the style and content of the marketing material.

The Registration Contact

Back to basics here. Registration should be made as easy as possible for your prospects. Although it might be possible for people to sign up for your seminar by mail, fax, or walk-in, they will most likely call you to register. This will be your first opportunity to initiate a personal relationship. The following checklist will guide you through the registration process.

Telephone Registration Checklist

1. Registration telephones are answered by you or one of your staff, rather than by an answering service or machine.   _____
2. Telephones are answered with a script to assure uniformity and quality.   _____
3. The individual answering the telephone is friendly and upbeat.   _____
4. Every caller is made to feel special and important.   _____
5. Each caller is treated as if he or she were already your client.   _____

Telephone Registration Script.   This is a sample script for handling incoming telephone registration calls for your seminar. This script should be modified for your particular audience and seminar topic.

All scripts should be delivered in a natural and conversational style. An effective script should never sound like one.

Registration Script

Step 1. Opening
Hello, this is (name of company), this is (name of person), speaking, how may I help you?

Step 2. Probing
Take down the registrant's name, address, and telephone number.

In order to make this seminar as valuable as possible for you, can I ask you a few questions?

First ask some general questions. For example:

How did you hear about this seminar?

What information would you like to get from this seminar?

Have you been to any other seminars like this?

What specific material would you like covered at this seminar?

Next ask some questions to begin to assemble a personal profile. These questions will be based upon your specific topic.

If your seminar is estate planning, some questions might be:

Have you taken any steps to protect your estate?

Are you aware of how much of your estate will be lost to taxes?

If the registrant feels comfortable, you can ask more personal questions such as:

How many children do you have?

How old are they?

Step 3. Confirmation and Benefit Assurance
We have you registered for (Name of seminar) on (Date). It will begin at (Time). It will be held at (Location).

Mr./Ms. (Name), I guarantee you'll profit from this seminar. Please feel free to call us anytime before this seminar with any specific problems you would like us to help you solve. We will be mailing you a written confirmation in the mail. We look forward to seeing you at the seminar. (If you'll be personally seeing them at the seminar say, I'm looking forward to meeting you at the seminar.)

You will be establishing your image and the way the registrants feel about you during the course of this dialogue. Don't minimize the importance of this first direct contact on the phone.

In some cases a simple written questionnaire can be used to gather information. Make sure it is nonthreatening. Don't ask questions that are too personal. General questions to uncover problems or concerns and questions that will reveal some background information, such as marital status, occupation, and retirement plans, are fine.

The Confirmation Letter

A confirmation letter should be sent out after the individual has registered for the seminar. This letter should again stress the benefits of the seminar. Make sure the letter is appropriate for your TADA. It should have the look and feel your target audience will relate to.

Sample Confirmation Letter

Stuart Financial Planning
79 West 33rd St.
New York, NY 10069

Dear (Name):

Congratulations on your enrollment in the _____
Seminar on (Date) at the (Location). We will be serving coffee and refreshments at (Time) and the seminar will begin at (Time).

We hope you are as excited about attending this event as we are about seeing you and sharing what could be the most valuable financial information you've ever received.

Sincerely,

Paul Stuart CFP
President

The Confirmation Phone Call

The confirmation phone call addresses two issues. First, it provides you with an additional personal contact with your seminar registrant. Second, it helps reduce no-shows at your seminar.

Large numbers of no-shows can threaten the success of your seminar, especially in large cities. A confirmation phone call one or two days prior to the seminar will substantially reduce your no-show rate.

Sample Confirmation Phone Call Script

Hello Mr./Ms. (Name). This is (Your name) with (Your company). I'm calling to confirm your registration for the _____ Seminar on (Day), (Date), at (Time), at (Location).

We have a limited number of seats and we wanted to make sure we'll be seeing you.

BUILD RELATIONSHIPS AT THE SEMINAR

Naturally, the seminar itself is the perfect environment to build relationships with your prospects. You will have the opportunity to share time in a relaxed environment. There are three parts to the event itself: before the seminar, the seminar itself, and after the seminar. Each part lends an optimal opportunity to establish relationships.

What to Do Before the Seminar Begins

Again, focusing on relationship building is the critical objective. The following guidelines will keep you focused on the participants and will make a successful first impression:

1. Introduce yourself and greet people as they arrive for the seminar.
2. Circulate among the participants and engage in light conversation.

3. Introduce individuals to each other and help them to feel comfortable.
4. Ask people what they would like to get out of the seminar.
5. Continue to probe and find out as much as you can about the participants.

What to Do During the Seminar

Treat your seminar participants with respect. Be likable and accessible. Your seminar should be a form of dialogue with your audience. Remember, you are taking on the role of a helpful consultant.

Caution: Never offend anyone, even if they are problem makers. You will lose your relationship with the rest of your audience. Conversely, if you show patience and understanding, you will draw the members of your audience closer to you.

What to Do After the Seminar Ends

Hopefully, in the course of the seminar you have brought out some important points, answered many questions, and raised some interesting ones in the minds of those attending your program. Often, however, people will want to talk to you further, so you should make yourself available to them after the seminar. Allow yourself at least one hour after each seminar to talk with members of your audience. You will build more rapport and your potential clients will feel more comfortable with you.

WII-FM?

If you want your seminars to result in new business, you must continually focus on answering your audience's question, "What's in it for me?"

All human behavior stems from two basic desires: to gain rewards or to avoid punishment. This can also be described as a desire to gain pleasure or avoid pain. Your relationship with the individuals who attend your seminar will grow if they identify you as a source who will help them gain their rewards.

Don't fall into the trap of becoming too involved in the features of your products and services instead of the benefits. Yes, you must provide practical financial information at your seminar to appear credible, but you must also relate the logic to their emotions every step of the way.

Karasik's Law of Sales

People buy for emotional reasons and justify with logic.

In other words, your advertisements, marketing material, references, analogies, and anecdotes during the seminar must continually refer back to the benefits your seminar and services will provide your participants.

For example, profitable investing is logical, but the peace of mind your prospects will have knowing their sons or daughters will be able to attend college is emotional.

Estate planning is logical, but the prospects' knowing their grandchildren will enjoy the money you have saved for them is emotional.

Retirement planning is logical, but your prospects' image of spending their last years in poverty is emotional.

Money is absolutely the bottom line at a financial seminar, but your focus should always be directed toward what that money can buy. It is the *emotions* associated with their money that will motivate your prospects to take action.

TWO INVALUABLE CLOSING TECHNIQUES

The seminar participant evaluation form and the "Ten Question Quiz" will enable you to sign individuals up for private consultations.

The Seminar Participant Evaluation

The participant evaluation is an opportunity for the individual to request a complimentary consultation. Distribute the evaluation at the end of the seminar, or, if it is in their materials, ask everyone to take it out. Explain to them the importance of filling out the evaluation and walk the participants through the form.

Sample Evaluation Form

Name _____   Occupation _____

Spouse's Name _____

Street _____

City _____   State _____   Zip _____

Home Phone _____   Business Phone _____

What did you like most about today's seminar?

_____

What idea did you find most valuable?

_____

☐ YES, I am interested in creating more wealth and would like to schedule a complimentary consultation.

☐ NO, I am not interested in a complimentary consultation.

My primary areas of interest are:

☐ Retirement planning   ☐ College funding
☐ Investment strategies   ☐ Estate planning
☐ Tax reduction   ☐ Portfolio review
☐ Asset allocation   ☐ Tax-advantaged investing

The Ten Question Quiz

The purpose of the Ten Question Quiz is to make the participants feel uncomfortable. Sow the seeds of discontent and you will motivate the participants to take action. Your Ten Question Quiz should be customized to your seminar topic, your audience, and your financial products and services.

The ideal time to ask the participants to take the quiz is just before a break. The quiz will motivate individuals to come up and speak with you at the break. This will give you an opportunity to build the relationship and set up an appointment for a consultation. The following are a few examples of sample questions for an estate planning seminar and a basic financial planning seminar.

Sample Questions for an Estate Planning Seminar

	Yes	No
1. Have you avoided the possibility of having some of your assets triple taxed at your death?	___	___
2. Are you sure you have avoided the estate tax on your life insurance?	___	___
3. Are you aware of the tax advantages of trusts?	___	___
4. Do you know how to give your corporate stock to your family and pay no gift tax?	___	___
5. Do you know how to enhance the power of your $600,000 estate tax exemption?	___	___

Sample Questions for an Basic Financial Planning Seminar

	Yes	No
1. Do you have a comprehensive investment strategy based upon your income needs and your personal goals and objectives?	___	___
2. Have you adequately provided for your family and yourself in the event of disability, retirement, or death?	___	___
3. Do you know how much discretionary income you can expect over the next five years?	___	___
4. Have you reviewed your life insurance coverage within the last two years to make sure you have adequate coverage?	___	___
5. Are you currently maximizing all of your tax-advantaged investments?	___	___

CLOSING AT YOUR COMPLIMENTARY CONSULTATION

Selling skills are essential to your success, regardless of your financial expertise and the quality of your financial products. The following is a simple sales process for closing the sale. Naturally, you should must customize your sales process according to your style.

Step 1. Make friends and establish rapport. When the prospect arrives, take some time to create a friendly environment. Show interest in the prospect and begin to gather information about her. Find out about her work, her family, her interests, sports or hobbies she enjoys, and so forth.

During this initial phase, convey to your prospect that you really care about him or her. Identify some areas of mutual interest and reveal a little about yourself.

Step 2. Acquire financial information. Get a good idea about the prospect's concerns and resources. Find out where the individual is now and where he or she wants to be in the future.

Step 3. Get specific. Using a questionnaire filled out by seminar participants, or using information the individual has brought to the consultation, gather the specific information you need to make your presentation.

Step 4. Make your presentation. Based upon the needs of the prospect and the information the prospect has shared, make your presentation.

Step 5. Ask for the order.

Sales studies reveal the necessity of developing a script. Once you find the words and flow that works for you, use it again and again.

Stay focused on building the relationship and avoid speaking in terms of the features of your products and services. Be generous and let people know you care about their finances and their lives, and you will master the art of closing the seminar sale.

Chapter Five

How to Design a Perfect Financial Seminar

The definition of a perfect seminar is simple: it satisfies the needs of those who attend it, and it results in new business for you.

Secret to a Perfect Seminar

Ask your target audience what they want and then give it to them.

ASSEMBLE YOUR MASTERMIND GROUP

A mastermind group is a circle of individuals that you can have a formal or informal commitment with that provides insights and information that will help you achieve your goals. Although your audience is one of the best sources of ideas on what to cover in your seminar, the following are a number of other resources you should include in your seminar design mastermind group:

1. Your target audience. Even before you have conducted your first seminar, you can ask members of your target audience for ideas.
2. Professional colleagues. People you work with and who sell similar financial products and services are good resources.
3. Teachers, instructors, and gurus. Anyone who currently teaches your topic will be familiar with the material people want to know.

4. Professional associations. Many professional associations provide educational material that includes useful statistics, research results, and background information that you can use when designing a seminar.

5. Your organization. More than likely, your organization already has published material on your topic. The marketing material produced by your organization is also likely to include lots of nuggets for your seminar.

6. Your sponsor. If your seminar is being sponsored by an organization, you should definitely ask them about any particular concerns they might have. For example, if your seminar is sponsored by an organization composed of senior citizens, you might ask them for some input.

USE INTERVIEWS TO FOCUS YOUR SEMINAR

Use simple oral and written interviews to determine what material would be most effective when included in your seminar. Be sure to keep accurate notes of the various interviews you conduct.

The following questionnaire is a guide for conducting oral or written interviews.

Sample Oral or Written Questionnaire

In order to present a powerful seminar program we need your help. We want to make sure we address your specific needs and help you solve your specific problems. Please answer the following questions.

What three things would you like covered in this seminar?

1. _____
2. _____
3. _____

If you could have only one of these three things, which would you choose and what would it mean to you?

_____
_____
_____

THE MODULAR DESIGN APPROACH (MDA) TO SEMINAR DESIGN

After collecting information from your mastermind group, you will have an overwhelming amount of information. The most effective technique for organizing this information is called the Modular Design Approach. The MDA is built upon the strategy of breaking down the seminar into small sections or modules. The advantages of the MDA include the following:

1. MDA creates bite-size blocks of information. Instead of designing a whole seminar at once, you can focus on much more manageable sections.
2. Modules can be stand-alone mini-seminars. For example, mutual funds could be a module of a money management seminar or it could be a seminar by itself.
3. MDA makes customizing your seminar easy. You can present your seminar as a full-day, half-day or one-hour presentation by simply adding or deleting modules. You can also rearrange the modules, depending on the needs of a particular audience.
4. Modules can later be packaged into other media, such as chapters of a book or sections of a video or audio series.

HOW TO IDENTIFY YOUR SEMINAR MODULES

One of the best ways to identify your seminar modules is to use a technique called "branching" (see Figure 5–1 for an illustration of this brainstorming technique). This technique very easy to learn. Here's how to do it:

1. Draw a circle in the middle of a sheet of paper and write the title of your seminar in it.
2. Based upon your research, write down topics that should be included in your seminar, branching these around the seminar title in the center of the page. Don't organize the information yet. Just get it down.

FIGURE 5–1

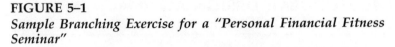
Sample Branching Exercise for a "Personal Financial Fitness Seminar"

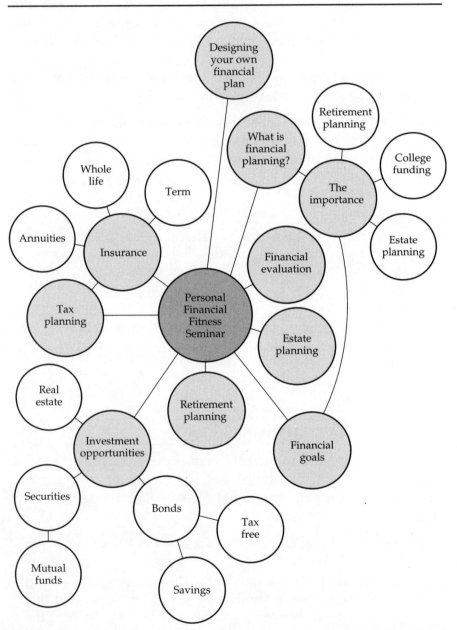

3. Continue to branch out other topics or ideas that relate to each of the ideas.

4. Now look at your sheet of paper, and connect the topics that belong together.

5. Determine what information should be organized under what module. You might find that some material falls under more than one module title, but that's OK. Organize your modules according to the specific needs of your audience and the overall topic of your seminar.

Figure 5–1 illustrates Steps 1–4 of a branching exercise for a financial planning seminar called "Personal Financial Fitness Seminar." The diagram in Figure 5–1 has identified the following modules of the seminar:

• What is financial planning.
• Setting your goals.
• Financial evaluation.
• Investment opportunities.
• Tax planning.
• Estate planning.
• Retirement planning.
• Insurance.
• Designing your own financial plan.

PRIORITIZE YOUR MODULES

Prioritizing your modules is very simple. Just ask yourself, If I could deliver just one of these modules, which one would it be? Then label that module "A."

After you have determined which is the most important module, ask yourself the same question about the remaining modules and label that one "B."

Repeat this process until you have prioritized all of your seminar modules. You might not need all the modules for every presentation, but using the MDA method will prepare you to deliver a well-designed seminar regardless of the format.

Because your seminar lengths may vary and because you may vary which modules you will include, it is important that each module have an opening, a body, and a closing. Let's say you must deliver a 50-minute presentation. Even if you include only the most important module or modules, you will still have a complete presentation. Remember, each individual module is structured like a seminar.

SEVEN WAYS TO MAKE YOUR CONTENT ROCK SOLID

The seven techniques that follow will help you make your seminar more impressive:

1. **Examples.** Use clear examples that your audience can relate to. Your example will transform an abstract or general idea into a concrete form and help you drive your point home. For example, at an estate planning seminar you might say something like, "Even though your estate is worth over a million dollars, your grandchild might only receive $200,000 after taxes."

2. **Case studies.** Case studies are perfect ways to personalize an example. They make your example come alive. Always include specific data that will help your audience envision the situation.

3. **Anecdotes.** Everybody enjoys a good story. Financial services seminars often get lost in numbers. Anecdotal stories add the human element. When you hear a good story, write it down. Keep a journal of stories you can use at your seminar.

4. **Statistics and figures.** It is difficult—if not impossible—to design a financial seminar without including lots of statistics and facts about finances. You should focus any statistics on your topic and keep them interesting and relevant. For example, "Over all 20-year periods from 1926 to the

present, U.S. government bonds kept pace with inflation only 28 percent of the time while stocks did 100 percent of the time."

5. **Definitions.** Be sure to define the terms you use throughout the seminar. If you have done your homework, you are aware of the sophistication of your audience and you will define only the necessary ones. If you are delivering a basic money management seminar, you will need to define many key terms.

6. **Research reports.** If you are discussing a particular financial product, be sure to include any independent studies or findings that support what you say about it.

7. **Authoritative sources.** The effect of including an authoritative source is similar to a research report: it identifies a third party. Third-party statements add credibility to any seminar because they make your claims and information seem more objective to your audience.

THE SECRET INGREDIENT TO YOUR SEMINAR

When you design your seminar, you must include audience participation. Your goal is to create a motivational event rather than a passive experience. Adults need to be actively engaged in the seminar experience.

The following list outlines the kinds of activities that work well in a financial seminar:

1. **Group questions.** You can ask the group, "How many people . . . ?" or "Can I see a show of hands . . . ?" Although this device can be overdone, it still gets a positive response when used.

   Caution: If you ask for a show of hands, be sure to acknowledge the response. If you don't, people will quickly lose interest in responding. You can say something like, "I can see most of you . . ." or "Thank you. That reinforces the need to . . ."

2. **Tests and quizzes.** People love to take quizzes. You can use these tests and quizzes to help people define or reflect on a personal need or idea they might have. The following is an example using a true or false format.

Personal Financial Fitness Exam

1. Both municipal and corporate bonds generate a
   tax-free income.   T or F
2. There are insurance products that generate tax-free
   income.   T or F
3. Over the long run stocks are a high risk investment.   T or F

---

3. **Fill in the blank workbooks.** Designing your seminar materials with lots of opportunities to write information in a workbook is an excellent way to keep your audience engaged.

4. **Small group discussions.** Breaking people up into small groups is a classic technique that creates lots of energy in the room. You can give people simple, nondemanding, nonthreatening topics to discuss. Even something as simple as what they would like to get out of the seminar will be a powerful addition to your seminar.

5. **Worksheets.** Ask your audience to calculate figures. This will make concrete an otherwise abstract concept.

HOW TO GET APPROVAL BY THE NATIONAL ASSOCIATION OF SECURITIES DEALERS

If you presenting an educational seminar on financial planning and you are not selling any financial products, there is no need to get any form of approval. On the other hand, if you are licensed to sell and intend to sell securities products, it will be necessary to get NASD approval for all your seminar and marketing materials through the compliance department of your company.

RESOURCES

The National Association of Securities Dealers, Inc., prefers all contacts with the organization be made by the broker/dealer rather than by the registered representative.

National Association of Securities Dealers Association, Inc.
Advertising Regulation Department
1735 "K" St. NW
Washington, DC 20006
(202) 728-8330
Fax (202) 728-6976

Chapter Six

Should You Buy a Prepackaged Seminar or Make Your Own?

There are a variety of debates that seem to go on forever in the business world: lease or buy, adjustable or fixed, stocks or bonds, foreign or domestic. Likewise, after you make your decision to conduct financial seminars, you will have to decide whether to buy a prepackaged seminar or design your own.

This information will help you decide which is the best choice for you.

THE PREPACKAGED SEMINAR

Prepackaged seminars are designed to be turn-key, ready-to-go seminars on a specific topic. All you need to add is yourself.

Most prepackaged seminars include a leader's guide or script, handouts, slides, and/or overhead transparencies. Some prepackaged seminars include marketing support such as brochures and camera-ready advertisements as well as user-group meetings.

Advantages of Prepackaged Seminars

The primary advantage of conducting prepackaged seminars is obvious. We live in an age of instant gratification. Everyone wants everything as fast as possible with as little effort as possible. Off-the-shelf seminars are the microwave alternative to taking the time and energy necessary when designing your own financial seminar.

Not only can individuals begin presenting financial seminars, entire teams of individuals can be mobilized simultaneously and consistently. If a district or regional office is seeking to capture a large market share, prepackaged seminars can be distributed and a fairly high level of quality control can be ensured.

Another advantage of the prepackaged seminar is the quality of the materials. Prepackaged seminars have been professionally designed, and in most cases, they have been field-tested by individuals like yourself and the "bugs" have been worked out. The content and format of the seminar design has been well thought out and specifically created for you to develop new business.

Disadvantages of Prepackaged Seminars

The primary and most serious disadvantage of prepackaged seminars is their generic nature. Although at first this might seem like a small trade-off, in reality this represents the primary reason the best-laid seminar-selling programs often fail to meet expectations.

The secret to successful marketing is the ability to identify and pursue a very specific target market. TADA is the ongoing dictum when seeking success in the seminar business. So while prepackaged seminars can be focused on one topic, in many cases they fall short in hitting the specific target audience.

For example, a preretirement seminar for doctors or dentists needs to be designed differently than a similar program for blue-collar workers. The prepackaged seminar does not speak the language of everyone. Remember, people who attend seminars want to feel confident you understand their specific needs and problems.

Another common problem with prepackaged seminars is a tendency for the presentation to sound "canned." This is the biggest danger associated with prepackaged seminars. If the individual attending the seminar does not get the impression that you are sincere, it is unlikely this person will want to become more involved with you.

Like any product, some prepackaged seminars are better than others. Some turn-key programs promise more than they actually deliver. The ideal product should include some follow-up and ongoing support components.

DESIGN YOUR OWN SEMINAR

Designing your own seminar is like buying a custom-made suit. The seminar is tailored to address the specific needs of your audience. Customized seminars have a TADA, and the workbooks, the visuals, and the entire program are designed especially for those attending your program. Customized seminars also conform to you and your personal presentation style.

Customized seminars generally "feel better" because they fit you and your audience like a glove. The customized seminar communicates to each member of the audience, "I know you and your financial challenges." Such seminars enable you to create an atmosphere that is more comfortable for you, and consequently, your audience, which substantially increases your effectiveness. Your relationship with your audience develops quickly because you use examples, case studies, and anecdotal stories they can identify with. You automatically build their confidence in you.

There is an old adage in sales: "People don't care how much, until they know how much you care." The customized seminar is the perfect vehicle to let your audience know how much you care about their financial needs.

The only major disadvantage of a customized seminar is that it requires an investment: of time, energy, or both. You can invest your own time or hire a consultant. But, like a customized suit, you make a better impression and feel better when you are delivering a seminar that you designed.

So, what's the answer? Which type of seminar is better? The answer is: It depends. If you are interested in a basic generic seminar, prepackaged will do just fine. If you will be conducting seminars for a specific target audience, you will need a more customized presentation.

THE COMBO PACKAGE

Customizing a prepackaged seminar might be the best route to take. Purchasing a turn-key program will get you going immediately, then you can slowly add and delete material according to your TADA and your personal presentation style.

Staying current and knowledgeable on available investment products, changes in tax laws, and so on, will allow you to modify the content of your program and continuously improve the content of your seminar.

Similarly, you must be able to develop the materials that will accompany the modifications and changes in your seminar. You need vendors who can produce your new slides, transparencies, workbooks, and marketing materials.

It is not necessary to modify your seminar every month, but your professionalism will be reflected in the presentation. If new laws are enacted that affect the content your seminar and you fail to include these changes, you will not be perceived as the expert and you will not win the trust of your participants.

HIRE A CONSULTANT

The final option for the financial industry professional is to hire a qualified consultant to design a customized seminar for you. The following guidelines will help you choose the right consultant and achieve the results you are looking for:

1. Decide on your goals and objectives beforehand. It is important to become clear on the results you are seeking. How many new clients would you like to develop? How many seminars a year would you like to conduct? Who is your target audience?

2. Find a consultant with industry experience. The financial industry has changed enormously over the last few years and will continue to change in the future. Don't expect a consultant from the furniture business to be able to speak your language, unless you are in the furniture business.

3. Find a consultant who is familiar with seminar design. It is essential that the consultant be familiar with the principles of seminar design. You don't want to pay for the consultant's learning experience.

4. Referrals are best. Ask colleagues first. If you belong to a professional association, call for a recommendation.

5. Make your decision based upon value rather than cost. As in most purchasing situations, you get what you pay for. Seek the best and you'll get a better return on your investment. You'll also avoid having to pay for the same job twice.

RESOURCES

Here is a list of suppliers of prepackaged financial seminars. These seminar programs vary in content, design, components, follow-up support, and pricing. It is well worth your time to contact these suppliers and review their products and services.

American Seminar Leaders Association
206 Sacramento St., Suite 201
Nevada City, CA 95959
(800) 735-0511
Fax (916) 965-2338

Dearborn Publishing Group, Inc.
520 N. Dearborn
Chicago, IL 60610
(800) 245-BOOK

Bill Good Marketing
P.O. Box 1959
Sandy, UT 84091-1959
(801) 572-1480

Emerald Publishing
11555 Rancho Bernardo Road
San Diego, CA 92127
(800) 233-2384

Financial Visions
8200 Humboldt Avenue South, Suite 215
Minneapolis, MN 55431
(612) 881-8292

Garrett Financial Group
1117 Hunters Chase Drive
Franklin, TN 37064
(615) 790-6791

Ibbotson Associates
225 North Michigan Avenue, Suite 700
Chicago, IL 60601-7676
(312) 616-1620
Fax (312) 616-0404

Marketing Masters, Inc.
4430 E. New York, Suite 133
Aurora, IL 60504
(800) 491-8736
Fax (708) 527-9239

Monstad and Christensen
P.O. Box 1709
Oak Harbor, WA 98277
(800) 654-1654

Successful Money Management
10180 S.W. Nimbus Avenue
Portland OR 97223
(800) 326-7667
Fax (800) 79-FAX-IT

Chapter Seven

How to Create Impressive Handout Materials

Your seminar materials and how they are assembled are a direct reflection on you and you should therefore produce them with care. Properly designed handout materials will result in more business.

THE IMPORTANCE OF HANDOUTS

There are a few good reasons to include some form of handout or workbook at your seminar.

1. **People expect them.** Most people have attended at least a few seminars and have received written material that reinforces the seminar. If you fail to provide some handout material, you will likely disappoint your participants.

2. **Handouts are a subtle form of advertising.** Your handout material will contain contact information, even it's just a mention of your company name and telephone number.

3. **Handouts indicate professionalism.** If you provide a well-thought-out handout or workbook, you will position yourself and your organization as a true professional.

4. **Handouts make an important contribution to helping you close the sale.** If your handouts help the participant realize a need for professional financial assistance, you will be leading the participant further along in the closing process.

5. **Handouts help create a positive experience for your participants.** You will win points with your participants when your handouts receive an active response, a humorous response, or even result in providing them with new ways of thinking.

WHAT YOUR HANDOUT *MUST* INCLUDE

The purpose of conducting your seminar is for you to initiate a relationship. Therefore, your handout must include a simple form that can facilitate the continuation of this relationship.

Your objective is to set up as many appointments with qualified individuals as possible. The easiest way to do this is to provide a seminar evaluation form that includes a request for more information or an appointment with you. Here's a simple yet very effective format you can use.

Financial Success Strategies

☐ Yes, please schedule me for a complimentary consultation.
☐ No, I am not interested right now.

WHAT YOUR HANDOUTS CAN INCLUDE

Don't be afraid to get creative when designing your handouts. You can mix and match. Great handouts can include one or more of the following items. In all cases, make sure you produce quality materials.

1. Quizzes, tests, and self-evaluations. As described in the Chapter 5, these components are perfect vehicles for creating participation at your seminar.

2. Fill-in-the-blank. Like quizzes and tests, you will keep your audience involved if you use the fill-in-the-blank format. You can

design your entire handout using this technique or simply use it to reinforce certain material.

3. Resource lists. Lists that provide other sources of helpful information (such as lists of specific types of mutual funds or government publications on tax regulations) are excellent to include and your participants will appreciate this extra effort to help them.

It may seem like you are educating yourself out of a job, but nothing is further from the truth. Providing this information for your prospects will result in one of three things: (1) the participants never bother following up and therefore still need your assistance; (2) they follow up, but realize they are not the expert so they still need your help; or, (3) they are impressed by your sincere desire to help them and you gain a significant amount of trust with your participants. Remember, gaining their trust is the first objective in achieving success.

4. Reprints. Articles that relate to your seminar topic are perfect handouts. Ideally, these articles should be written by you. Be sure to get permission to reproduce material that is copyrighted.

5. Gimmicks and freebies. There is an old adage in selling, "Give away something for free." Years ago salespeople would give away a fine pen to a prospect. The give-away technique is as effective today as it was then. Of course, it is important that your item be relevant. Anything from a humorous bumper sticker to well-designed folio will leave a very positive impact.

6. Books. Statistics have proven that most people have read only 10–20 percent of the books on their bookshelf, yet most people have tremendous difficulty throwing a book away. Books contribute to the perceived value of your seminar.

Naturally, the best book is one written by you. If you haven't written a book, you should distribute a book that endorses your views or approach to the topic. You can get copies of most books by contacting the publisher directly.

7. Copies of your visuals. Hard copy of your slides or transparencies are the least effective handout you can distribute. The reason is simple: it looks like you didn't take a lot of time in preparing your handout.

Although this type of handout material can provide a comprehensive outline of your program it appears to be a quick fix. If you do intend to use your visuals as handout material, you should expand them and provide more details within the framework of the text or graphics.

HOW TO ASSEMBLE YOUR HANDOUTS

There are a few ways to design handouts for your seminar. Examine your alternatives and then choose the style that fits your particular target.

Three-Ring Binder

The three-ring binder is an excellent format if you are delivering a program that is one-half day or longer. Three-ring binders are available in a variety of sizes. The most appropriate sizes are the one-half-inch and one-inch ring.

Three-ring binders are available with clear overlay covers at your local discount stationery store. You can insert a sheet of standard 8 1/2 × 11" paper into the clear overlay and you have an instant cover. Or, you might want to imprint the covers.

The three-ring-binder approach also allows you to retain flexibility. Using MDA (modular design approach), you can separate each module with index tabs and add or delete material within the module.

Important: If you are using a three-ring binder workbook, number your pages by the module. (For example, module 1 would be numbered 1–1, 1–2, 1–3, and so on. Module 2 would be numbered 2–1, 2–2, 2–3, and so on.) This system allows you to revise one module without disturbing the other modules.

Bound Workbooks

The three primary ways to bind your workbooks are: stapled booklets, spiral plastic comb binding, and perfect binding. Although stapled booklets are the most inexpensive, there is not that big a difference in the cost. You should make your decision based on the cost, length, and format of your particular seminar—and of course, your TADA or target audience. If your market is upscale, you will want to invest in top-of-the-line handouts and bindings. Similarly, if your seminar is only an hour or two in length, a well-printed two or three-page color booklet will work well.

Your local printer can probably handle a small run of stapled workbooks or spiral plastic comb binding, but if you are looking for the best price, check the specialty printers listed at the end of this chapter.

Perfect binding is "book style." This is the most impressive format, especially if you have an effective cover. The main disadvantage of the perfect binding format is you will have no flexibility in adding or deleting material.

Folder

The folder format allows for maximum flexibility. If you want to amend your handout in any way, you simply add or delete the materials you are inserting in the folders. You can insert single sheets or even slip a workbook into the folder.

You also can custom design your folder by imprinting your company logo, and name of your seminar on it. This will add to the impact and create a professional look. See the list below for companies that specialize in custom-designed folders.

RESOURCES

Here are some excellent resources for supplying you with products, services, and expertise to ensure the highest quality handout materials.

The following companies specialize in customized binders.

American Thermoplastic Company
106 Gamma Drive
Pittsburgh, PA 15238-2949
(800) 245-6600

Creative Vinyl Products
2600 United Lane
Elk Grove Village, IL 60007
(708) 766-2430

Colad Inc.
701 Seneca Street
Buffalo, NY 14210
(716) 849-1776

DVC Industries
1440 Fifth Avenue
Bayshore, NY 11706
(800) 968-8500

Reliance Plastics
217 Brook Avenue
Passaic, NJ 07055
(201) 473-1023

Vinylweld
2011 W. Hastings
Chicago, IL 60608
(800) 444-4020

The following companies specialize in a variety of do-it-yourself handout materials. Using the well-designed folders and presentation materials they provide and simple computer programs, you can produce very sophisticated handout material for your seminar.

Paper Direct
205 Chubb Avenue
Lyndhurst, NJ 07071
(800) A PAPERS

Queblo
1000 Florida Avenue
Hagerstown, MD 21741
(800) 523-9080

The following printers specialize in booklets and short-run perfect bound books.

Triangle Printing
325 Hill Avenue
Nashville, TN 37210
(800) 843-9529

Dinner + Klein
600 South Spokane Street
Seattle, Washington 98134
(206) 682-2494

Crane Duplicating Service, Inc.
1611 Main Street
West Bramble, MA 02668
(508) 362-3441

Bookmasters
638 Jefferson Street
Ashland, OH 44805
(800) 537-6727

The following companies specialize in producing custom-printed folders.

Folder Factory
116-A High Street
Edinburg, VA 22824
(800) 368-5270

Artline Industries
3091 Governors Lake Drive
Norcross, GA 30071
(800) 662-0101

Chapter Eight

How to Choose and Use Audiovisuals

WHY YOU SHOULD USE VISUAL AIDS

The University of Minnesota and The Wharton School of Business at the University of Pennsylvania conducted an extensive study examining the effect of visuals on a presentation.[1] They concluded that presentations that included visuals were:

More persuasive.

Evaluated as higher quality.

Perceived as more professional.

These are some powerful reasons to include visuals in your seminar. But there a few other benefits of using visuals as well, such as the following.

1. Visuals will save you time. You've heard the old adage, "A picture is worth a thousand words." In most cases, your financial seminar will be limited in time, and visuals will allow you to cover more material in less time.

2. Visuals can clarify complex material. Presenting a visual will allow your audience to understand a point that can otherwise sound very complex.

3. Visuals will keep the attention of your audience. You must maintain the interest of your audience throughout your

---

[1] *Creative Training Techniques Handbook*, by Robert Pike, Lakewood Books, 50 S. Ninth Street, Minneapolis, MN 55402.

presentation, or else you will have extreme difficulty closing the sale.

HOW TO CHOOSE THE BEST VISUAL AID

There are four forms of visual aids that are appropriate for financial seminars: slide projectors, overhead projectors, flipcharts, and
marker boards. As always, make your decision based upon your
TADA and the logistics of your seminar. Use the following guidelines to decide which visual aid is best for you.

Slide Projector

Advantages.   Perfect for high resolution color graphics,
effective with extremely large groups, good for more formal situations.

Disadvantages.   Lack flexibility, hard to adjust if there is
a problem, not good for an interactive format, requires a fairly
dark room, custom slides can be expensive.

When to use.   When you want to present a one-way type
of presentation, slides are excellent. Once you are totally familiar
with the sequence you can deliver a presentation that is very pol-
ished. Also, if you are presenting your seminar in settings such
as a corporate setting, boardroom, or auditorium, slides work
well.

Tips for using the slide projector

1. Run through your slides before every presentation.
2. Make sure there is a spare bulb in the projector.
3. Use a wireless remote to maximize mobility.
4. Use a rear screen projection whenever possible. This will
   allow you to keep the house lights up and the screen will
   still be visible.

Overhead Projector

Advantages.   Versatile, easy to use, works well in a variety of settings, house lights can be left on, transparencies can be drawn during the seminar or prepared beforehand, any written material can be transferred to a transparency using a copy machine, inexpensive to create new transparencies.

Disadvantages.   Not as polished-looking as slides, projector limits mobility, does not work well with extremely large groups.

When to use.   Use overhead projectors when you want to emphasize the educational aspect of your presentation. Overhead projectors allow you to work in a well-lit room, enabling the audience to read and take notes.

Tips for using an overhead projector

1. Stand to the side of the projector.
2. Shut the projector off when you are not using it.
3. Use a pen or pencil to point to information.
4. Use the upper portion of the screen.
5. Mount the transparencies on cardboard frames.

Flipchart and Marker Board

Advantages.   Very flexible, allows for spontaneity.

Disadvantages.   Effectiveness is limited to groups of 50 or less, appearance is dependent upon your handwriting, requires time during seminar to write and/or erase.

When to use.   Flipcharts and marker boards are best when used in conjunction with a slide projector or overhead projector. They can add flair, variety, and life to your seminar. For example, you can use one of these visual aids to demonstrate how to calculate a specific financial example.

Tips for using flipcharts, whiteboards, and blackboards

1. Lightly pencil information on flipcharts before you begin.
2. Use a variety of color pens.
3. Prepare some of your flipchart or marker board in advance.
4. Avoid writing on the lower third of flipcharts and marker boards, for it is often difficult to see this area from the back of the room.

GUIDELINES FOR USING ALL VISUAL AIDS

The following is a list of basic techniques, rules, and tricks of the trade that maximize the effectiveness of your visuals and make you appear totally professional when presenting your seminar:

1. Make sure your visuals can be seen from all seats. The best way to do this is to set up your screen and then sit down in various parts of the room. When you are using a projector, place the screen to the right or the left of the staging area. This will prevent you from blocking the view of your participants.
2. Do not crowd slides or transparencies with too many words. Use the 6 × 6 rule: No more than six lines with a maximum of six words per line.
3. If you are showing graphs or charts, keep them simple.
4. Never use typewritten text. Use 18 point or larger type size.
5. When using a projector, do not project an empty screen. The glare it will create is annoying and unprofessional.
6. Don't fall into the habit of turning your back to the audience when using visuals. For all presentation techniques using visuals, use the "Turn, Touch, Talk" Technique discussed later on in this chapter.
7. Unscrew any lights that are shining on the screen. This technique will allow you to keep the house lights up and keep the screen dark. If the room has adjustable lights, be sure to turn them away from the screen.

8. If an audiovisual company, the hotel, or your seminar sponsor will be setting up the equipment for you, draw a diagram of how you would like the equipment set up. Be sure to include any tables you need to hold materials.

9. If you are using meeting facilities, standard audiovisual equipment will be available and it is usually much more convenient to order what you need. If you are presenting in places such as employee lunch rooms or restaurants, you might want to invest in the equipment you use to maintain quality control.

10. Always have plan B. It is possible that everything that can go wrong does with visuals. Even if the equipment is working and there is no power blackout, you might get to the seminar site and realize you've forgotten your slides or overhead transparencies. Plan B is a seminar with no visuals. Always be prepared for this possibility at any point in the presentation. Experience has proven that at some point in time, you will need to rely on a Plan B.

Deciding which equipment to use will depend on your audience, location, content, and personal delivery style. Regardless of which equipment you use, be sure to get continual feedback from others on how effective your audiovisuals are.

With the help of feedback and a professional attitude, you will be harnessing simple technology and making your presentation vastly more professional in no time at all. More importantly, you will make it vastly more persuasive.

RESOURCES

The following are some excellent resources for creating excellent professional visuals for your seminars.

Visual Horizons is an excellent one-stop for all of your audiovisual needs. You can find overhead projectors, slide projectors, screens, flipcharts, and just about every conceivable piece of presentation paraphernalia. Visual Horizons also has ready-made and made-to-order slides and overhead transparencies. Write or call for their free catalog.

Visual Horizons
180 Metro Park
Rochester, NY 14623-2666
(716) 424-5300
Fax (716) 424-5313

Cinegraph Communications specializes in fax slides. You fax them what you want on your custom slides, and they will ship them to you within 25 hours. Both their quality and prices are excellent. Write or call for their slide order forms.

Cinegraph Communications, Inc.
11642 Knott Ave., Bldg. #14
Garden Grove, CA 92641-1820
(714) 895-5298
Fax (714) 895-2160

National Underwriter Company produces a series of color slides especially for financial services seminars called "Field Guide Slides To Estate Planning, Business Planning, and Employee Benefits." The slides are accompanied by the appropriate script.

National Underwriter Company
505 Gest Street
Cincinnati, OH 45203-1716
(800) 543-0874
Fax (800) 874-1916

There are a variety of inexpensive software packages that enable you to produce professional-looking visuals, including BP's *Presentation Express,* Microsoft's *Powerpoint,* SP's *Harvard Graphics,* and Aldus' *Persuasion.* You can produce overhead transparencies on your laser printer or send your computer disk to a slide production company. Brilliant Image can produce your slides overnight.

Brilliant Image
Seven Penn Plaza
New York, NY 10001
(212) 736-9661

THE "TURN, TOUCH, TALK" TECHNIQUE

Many amateur presenters put up a slide or an overhead transparency on the screen and proceed to talk to the screen. The proper professional technique is to use the three part "Turn, Touch, Talk" Technique when you use a visual.

Step 1. Turn your body towards the visual you are presenting.

Step 2. Touch the visual with a pointer or point with an open palm to where you want the audience to focus its attention.

Step 3. When you begin to speak, talk to an individual in the audience.

This technique allows you to get the most from your visual while maintaining contact with your audience. Remember, your primary objective is to make contact with your audience and build your relationship.

PUTTING THE AUDIO INTO YOUR AUDIOVISUALS

One of the most overlooked elements that can add power and pizzazz to your seminar is the audio element. Audio equipment for seminars is composed of three primary elements: microphones, sound systems, and tape recorders for prerecorded sound.

Unless your group is less than 30 people, you should plan to use a microphone. If you are not blessed with a powerful voice, you may even want to use a microphone for smaller groups. Microphones serve a variety of functions, including the following:

1. Add power to your voice. A microphone ensures that you are heard equally throughout the room. Without one, the people sitting farthest from you may not hear you well.

2. Provide you with a dynamic range. Microphones enable you to add dynamics to your vocal delivery.

3. Preserve your voice. If you are delivering multiple seminars, you will add stress to your vocal chords if you do not use a microphone. Microphones help keep your voice in top shape.

4. Add vocal presence to your performance. A strong presence will contribute greatly to your persuasiveness. Microphones make you "larger than life" and fill the room vocally.

THE FOUR STYLES OF MICROPHONES

There are four styles of microphones to choose from: wired handheld, wireless handheld, wired lavaliere, and wireless lavaliere. (See Figure 8–1.) Because your gestures and movement compose a fairly large component of your visual presentation, having your mobility limited by a wire can severely reduce your

FIGURE 8–1
Microphone Styles

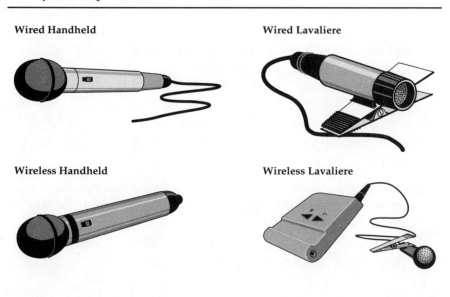

Wired Handheld

Wired Lavaliere

Wireless Handheld

Wireless Lavaliere

effectiveness. Therefore, the wired handheld and wired lavaliere are less desirable.

Why lose points on the easy stuff? When you are presenting a financial seminar, you need to equip yourself for optimum performance possibilities. The wireless lavaliere is your best choice. It will give you total freedom of movement and will leave both hands free to gesture, hold a workbook, point to a visual, or whatever. It is well worth the investment and will save you lots of money in microphone rentals.

GUIDELINES FOR USING MICROPHONES AND SOUND SYSTEMS

There is nothing more frustrating to a seminar audience than trying to hear an inaudible speaker. In almost every situation, this can be avoided by sticking to the following rules:

1. Arrive at your seminar room well in advance and test the equipment you will be using. If you are using your own microphone, test it in the house system to make sure it is compatible.
2. Introduce yourself and make friends with the person in charge of the audio equipment. This individual can end up making a big contribution to the success of your seminar, especially if there is a problem.
3. Walk around the room to check for any spots that produce feedback or a hum. This will show you which sections of the room you should avoid.
4. Always allow for the sound absorption factor of the audience. If you have tested the equipment in an empty room, be sure to turn up the volume between 10 and 20 percent when it is filled with people.
5. When using a wired microphone, be sure there is enough cord to allow you to move about freely. Additional cord length is usually available upon request.
6. If you are using a handheld microphone, make sure to hold it 6 to 8 inches away from your mouth.

7. Lavaliere microphones should be clipped on your garment as close as possible to your mouth.

8. Always put your wireless microphone into the standby mode when you are off the platform to avoid having private comments overheard by your audience.

9. Whenever possible, keep a wired microphone on hand as a back-up. Wireless microphones have been known to work fine during the test but then pick up some static during the seminar.

10. As with any equipment: test, test, and test one more time.

TAPE RECORDERS AND CD PLAYERS FOR USING PRERECORDED SOUND

An excellent addition to a seminar is background music during breaks and during networking portions of your event.

For optimum quality assurance, bring your own portable cassette deck or CD player. The small dual speaker portable sound system can work quite well for groups as large as 100, and you can practice with and test your equipment at your convenience.

You can also connect your player to the sound system quite easily. If you tell the audiovisual person beforehand the type of plug you need, he or she will usually have it ready when you arrive.

In some cases, there will be no house sound system. If you will be presenting seminars in locations that do not have sound systems, you should consider investing in a professional portable sound system that can serve multiple functions. These sound systems can be used to amplify your voice and provide a source for music amplification.

RESOURCES

The American Seminar Leaders Association can provide you with first-class wireless microphones and sound systems at excellent prices.

American Seminar Leaders Association
206 Sacramento Street
Suite 201
Nevada City, CA 95959
(800) 735-0511

FINAL ADVICE ON AUDIOVISUAL EQUIPMENT

You don't have to be a "techie" or a sound engineer to choose and use audiovisual equipment like a true professional seminar leader. Initially, you must understand the importance of the equipment you are using and how it affects the perception of your audience. Equipment used in an unprofessional manner can greatly diminish your closing ratios. You must also familiarize yourself with a full range of audiovisual possibilities so that you can adapt and modify according to the particular logistics of the seminar you are delivering. There is no one right choice for financial seminars. As in all choices, TADA is the guiding strategy.

Finally, make a commitment to developing your own individual audiovisual techniques. Anyone can master the techniques outlined in this chapter. It is essential to appear in control and professional in all aspects of your financial seminar, including your audiovisual equipment.

Chapter Nine

Choosing the Time and Place of Your Seminar

G ood timing and location are critical to the success of your program. There is no way to determine the best time and place without considering your TADA. When scheduling your seminar, consider the guidelines in this chapter.

CHECK YOUR CALENDAR

Before choosing the dates of your seminar, check the calendar for conflicts of any kind. The following are major conflicts to avoid:

1. Holidays. Never plan to hold a seminar directly before or after a holiday. This includes national, regional, local, and religious holidays.
2. National events. Be sure to avoid conflicts with major sporting events, political conventions, and so forth.
3. Local events. Watch out for events such as local fairs and sporting events.

BEST MONTHS AND DAYS OF THE WEEK

Of course, use TADA as your guide. Don't plan a seminar for accountants during the end of March or beginning of April, and don't promote a seminar for teachers on a weekday. However, if you are presenting a tax planning seminar for the general public, March would be a logical choice.

The following are general guidelines for choosing the best month and day of the week:

1. Early fall and early spring tend to be planning times for most people. These are also times when people want to get out to socialize and network. Research has shown that the autumn months of September and October and the spring months of April and May are the best months for seminars.

   Seminars during the winter months are fine, although you might lose attendance due to poor weather conditions if you are located in northern regions.

2. Generally, the best weekdays to hold seminars are Tuesday, Wednesday, and Thursday. Saturday is the best day of the weekend to present your seminar.

CHOOSING THE BEST TIME OF DAY

Here are some guidelines for scheduling the time of your seminar.

1. Half-day seminars should be scheduled between 8 AM and 12 PM or 1 PM and 5 PM. By scheduling these hours, you will avoid the necessity of serving a meal.

2. Full-day seminars should be scheduled between the hours of 8 AM and 5 PM. People schedule their days around these hours and you are likely to get fewer conflicts.

3. Evening seminars are best when scheduled between 5 PM and 9:30 PM. If you are serving dinner or refreshments, you can start between 5 PM and 6 PM. If you are not serving any food, it is best to start at 6 PM or 6:30 PM to allow people time to have dinner before attending the seminar.

PROVIDE AN ALTERNATE CHOICE

The best strategy for avoiding no-shows is to provide a choice. This will substantially increase your return on your investment.

Here's an example: Give your audience the choice of Wednesday at 1 PM or 6 PM, or Saturday at 9 AM or 1 PM. This strategy will add little to your expenses but will reduce your no-shows considerably. This way, if someone registers for a Wednesday seminar and fails to show up, you can contact this person on Thursday and offer him or her the opportunity to attend the Saturday seminar.

In some cases, you can even create a third day for the no-shows from the other two days. Enroll the no-shows on Wednesday and Saturday into a newly scheduled event one day the following week.

CHOOSING THE BEST SEMINAR SITE

Check the calendar of events in your newspapers and make a list of the sites currently being used for seminars in your area. As you collect names of possible venues, call them up and find out the room rental rates.

Consider the following points when selecting your seminar site:

1. Convenience. If your target audience is located downtown during the day, you will want to choose a location that is nearby and perhaps within walking distance.

2. Parking. If participants will be driving to your seminar, make sure there is adequate parking space.

3. Image. What kind of image do you want to create? If you are presenting a seminar on wealth-building through wise investment decisions, you will want to choose an upscale location.

Be sure to conduct an on-site inspection. There is no substitute for walking around a potential site and examining the location firsthand. The following checklist will help you inspect a seminar site.

Checklist for the Seminar Site

	Yes	No
Are the public areas neat and clean?	___	___
Are personnel courteous and efficient?	___	___
Is the banquet department service-oriented?	___	___
Is the temperature of the meeting rooms comfortable?	___	___
Are the chairs and tables comfortable?	___	___
Are the meeting rooms sufficiently soundproof?	___	___
What audiovisual equipment is included?	___	___
Who is the audiovisual equipment supplier?	___	___
What amenities such as pencils, pads, and so forth are included?	___	___
What is the cost of food and beverages?	___	___
Is there a restaurant on site?	___	___

RESOURCES

See the *Financial Seminar Leaders Resource Guide* for a complete list of excellent sites for financial seminars. This list is especially helpful if you are planning to hold seminars throughout the country.

Gavel and *SourceBook* are two directories that include information on thousands of hotels throughout the United States and the world.

Gavel
Meetings and Conventions
500 Plaza Drive
Secaucus, NJ 07096
(201) 902-1700
Fax (201) 319-1796

SourceBook
Successful Meetings
355 Park Avenue South
New York, NY 10010
(212) 592-6403
Fax (212) 592-6409

HOW TO MINIMIZE MEETING ROOM EXPENSES

Depending on your location, meeting-room and food and beverage charges can be very expensive. Heed the following tips to keep your expenses to a minimum:

1. Order coffee by the gallon instead of by the serving.
2. If you order soft drinks or juices, asked to be charged by consumption.
3. Always negotiate the room rental based on your repeat business.
4. Ask for the room-rental fees to be waived completely if the site is catering the event.

THE MEETING ROOM CONFIRMATION LETTER

Always mail or fax a room-confirmation letter to the facility. This will streamline the process and make it easier for the facility to serve you. Enclose your room set-up with this letter. Use the following sample letter as a format.

Sample Meeting Room Confirmation Letter

YOUR LETTERHEAD

Date

To: Contact Name
        Address

This letter confirms the details for our upcoming seminar, entitled

_____.

The date of this event is _____.

The hours are _____ to _____.

Please list the seminar as _____.

Set up the room for _____ people.

The food and beverage service is as follows:
Time: _____.
Food: _____.   Quantity _____.
Beverage: _____.   Quantity _____.

Please see the enclosed diagram for the location of chairs and tables.

Please see the enclosed list for our audiovisual requirements.

Thank you for your assistance helping us to make our seminar successful. Please call with any questions.

Sincerely,

Samantha Cara
Samantha Cara

Chapter Ten

How to Produce Winning Marketing Material

Evaluating the effectiveness of your seminar marketing material is simple: if it gets people to sign up for your seminar, it's first class. Regardless of how good it looks and how much money you spent producing it, the response rate is your ultimate measuring stick.

THE THREE PRIMARY FORMATS

Practically all financial seminar direct mail falls into one of three types of formats: the classic seminar brochure, the letter package, and the invitation style.

Regardless of which format you decide to use, here are the strategies and techniques you need to know to be able to create quality marketing material.

Follow these guidelines and you will create will create a seminar marketing piece that gets a good response.

RESOURCES

Here are two companies that can provide a very unique product line. They produce beautifully designed blank brochures. All you need to do is fill in your information. They even print return postcards that are perfect for mail-in registrations.

BeaverPrints
Main Street
Bellwood, PA 16617
(800) 923-2837
Fax (800) 232-8374

Idea Art
P.O. Box 291505
Nashville, TN 37229-1505
(800) 433-2278
Fax (800) 435-2278

FOCUS ON YOUR TARGET AUDIENCE

When deciding what types of marketing materials to use, you must again consider your TADA. If your seminar is geared toward members of a local union, you can keep your material pretty simple and inexpensive. On the other hand, if your seminar is directed toward the affluent, you will want to produce marketing material that will speak to their taste.

When delivering seminars to a variety of target audiences, you might want to consider using several different designs and approaches. You won't have to start from scratch with each piece, rather it will be more of an exercise in adapting your material for each particular target audience. Get in the habit of examining your marketing material through the eyes of the person who will be receiving it. If you do this, you are sure to receive a successful response.

HOW TO WRITE HOT COPY

Even if you are not a great writer, you'll be able to produce solid marketing material if you apply some very simple sales principles.

1. Focus on benefits. Yes, it's back to Selling 101. People buy to gain rewards or to avoid punishment. People will attend your seminar for the same reasons.

Remember, people who attend financial seminars need to solve problems. When creating your marketing materials, then, you can even state the problem first. This is a technique in sales called "touch the pain." For example you might say, "Did you know your assets may be *triple-taxed* at your death?" Then clearly state how your seminar will teach attendees the solution to this problem.

2. Repeat the benefits. Don't be afraid to repeat the benefits as many times as possible throughout the marketing material. For example you might say, "Register for this seminar today and you will learn the specific steps you can take to eliminate paying thousands of dollars in taxes."

You can never have too many benefits in a brochure, nor can you can you ever restate them too many times. All too often, marketing material copy *implies* rather than *states* the benefits. Naturally, you will want to mention what topics will be discussed at your financial seminar, but don't forget to mention why those topics are important to the prospect.

3. Keep it simple. It was once said that a good brochure can be understood by an eight-year-old. A good way to evaluate your marketing material copy is to ask yourself, "Is this easy to understand?"

Let's face it, a financial seminar is geared toward either saving money, making money, or keeping the money one has saved or made, so you should be able to sum up what your seminar is about in just a few words. Choosing a good title for your financial seminar will help you accomplish this.

4. Use short phrases, sentences, and paragraphs. Most people do not speak in long, punctuated sentences—they speak in short, conversational ones. The copy on your marketing material should be written in the same style.

Regardless of the format you use, you should use a "bullet" style whenever possible because it is the easiest and most interesting to read. For example, if you are presenting an investment seminar titled, "The Secrets to Financial Planning," your copy might read like this:

This seminar will include the following topics:

- Getting Started
- Wealth Accumulation
- Funding a College Education
- Buying a New Home
- Insuring Against Risk
- Planning for a Secure Retirement

5. Use powerful, direct words. Since you have space limitations, make sure you choose your words carefully. The following is a list of words you could include that are both powerful and direct:

Achieving	Maximize
Assessing	Measuring
Benefiting	Motivating
Building	Negotiating
Capitalize	New
Cash-in	Optimize
Confirm	Pinpoint
Conquering	Powerful
Create	Practical
Dealing	Probe
Diagnose	Profit
Easy	Profile
Eliminating	Proven
Expanding	Quick
Explode	Receive
Exploring	Results
Focusing	Save
Free	Sharpen
Fundamentals	Shatter
Gain	Step-by-Step

Grasp	Strategic
Guarantee	Tackle
Implementing	Target
How to	Tested
Increase ✓	Uncover
Influencing	Understand
Investing	Unlocking
Master ›	Why

RESOURCES

The following two invaluable books will assist you in writing great marketing copy: *Words That Sell,* by Richard Bayan (Caddylak Publishing, 201 Montrose Rd., Westbury, NY 11590), and *The Copywriter's Handbook,* by Robert W. Bly (Henry Holt and Company, 115 West 18th St., New York, NY 10011).

WHAT TO INCLUDE IN YOUR BROCHURE OR MARKETING MATERIAL

Consider the following items when you design your marketing material. You will probably not use all of them, but if you cross-reference your marketing material with this list, you'll be guaranteed to have a complete piece.

Promotional Materials Checklist

- ☐ Title. Choose a title that speaks to your TADA. Make it clear, direct, and easy to understand. Ideally, your title should convey a benefit. Titles like "Safe Money" and "How to Financially Prepare for Your Retirement" can work well.

- ☐ Hook. A hook is a subtitle that will restate benefits or further describe your program. Again, focus this hook on your TADA. Hooks such as, "Safeguard now for your children's education," or "Creating the retirement you've always dreamed of" will restate benefits.

☐ Dates, times, and location. More than one seminar leader has printed thousands of brochures without this information.

Save Money

If you are using a brochure format, include the date, location, and time in a box. Ask the printer to print the number of copies you need for the first seminar, then "burn off" this information and continue to print enough brochures for future seminars. When you need brochures in the future, all you have to do is print the date, location, and time in the box. You will save an enormous amount of money by using this technique.

☐ Who should attend. It is always a good idea to state who your target audience is right on the marketing material. For example, if your seminar is for small business owners, you can simply state, "This is a financial seminar for small business owners." Or, you could include it in the copy in a more indirect manner by saying, "Owning your own business can create some unique financial problems."

☐ Benefits. Seminars are, by definition, about benefits. People are attending your seminar to gain rewards or to avoid punishment. Therefore, rather than discussing features, your promotional material should reiterate benefits in many different ways and as many times as possible.

☐ What you will learn. This is a list of specific topics that will be discussed in your seminar. Use powerful words and action verbs and list the precise strategies and techniques your participants will learn.

☐ Program schedule. If you are presenting a program of a half-day or longer, you might want to provide a more complete agenda. If you are presenting a multi-day program, it is important to let individuals know what will be covered on what day.

☐ Client list. If you are delivering your seminars at corporations or for non-profit organizations, your credibility will be enhanced by providing a list of organizations who have benefited from your seminar. If you are brand new at seminar selling, you can still say something like, "Members of the following organizations have benefited from the information offered in this program." Then list employers of clients you have helped.

☐ Endorsements. Quotes by specific people who have taken your seminar should be listed. Be sure to include their name, profession or company, title, and the specific benefit they received. Here's where TADA becomes important once again.

☐ Seminar leader biography. Answer the question, "What makes you qualified to speak on this topic and to this audience?" The best biography is one that contains only the answer to this question and nothing else. People do not care about your pets—they want to know how you can help them with their financial planning!

Be sure to include any information that adds credibility to you as a seminar leader. For example, if you are a member of the American Seminar Leaders Association or are a Certified Seminar Leader, mention those facts in your bio.

☐ Your picture. Although a photo is not essential, an executive style photo is a nice addition to your materials.

☐ What will be included with the seminar? Are you providing any workbooks, checklists, audio tapes, reference material, financial health quizzes, and so forth? Any feature that might add value to your program should be stated in your marketing materials.

☐ Methods of payment. If there is a charge for your seminar, let people know how they can pay for it. List the credit cards you accept and to whom the checks should be made out.

☐ 800 numbers. It is simple and very inexpensive to set up an incoming 800 number that will ring on your regular telephone. If people will be calling from a variety of area codes to register for your seminar, it is a good idea to offer 800 service.

RESOURCES

The following three services can help you set up an 800 number.

AT&T
(800) 222-0400

MCI Telecommunications
(800) 888-0800

Sprint
(800) 877-4000

☐ How to register. Provide detailed instructions on how to sign up for the seminar. As discussed in Chapter 4, you can offer telephone, mail, fax, or register-at-the-door methods.

For more ideas on writing and designing promotional material, see "Eight Rules for Creating a Successful Newspaper Ad" in Chapter 12.

THE THREE MOST SUCCESSFUL DIRECT-MAIL APPROACHES

The three most common styles of direct mail marketing materials are the standard brochure, the letter invitation, and the wedding style invitation.

The Brochure

Brochures work well when promoting a financial seminar that is more than one to two hours in length and you are charging for the seminar.

Here is an example of a brochure for a one-day basic financial planning seminar. The brochure is printed on 11" × 17" and folded to 8 1/2" × 11" and then folded once again to 5 1/2" × 8 1/2". By folding it twice mailing costs will be the same as a regular first class letter.

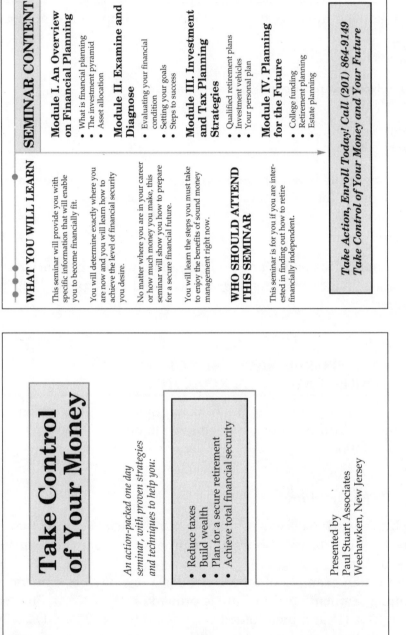

Take Control of Your Money

An action-packed one day seminar, with proven strategies and techniques to help you:

- Reduce taxes
- Build wealth
- Plan for a secure retirement
- Achieve total financial security

Presented by
Paul Stuart Associates
Weehawken, New Jersey

Brochure Cover

WHAT YOU WILL LEARN

This seminar will provide you with specific information that will enable you to become financially fit.

You will determine exactly where you are now and you will learn how to achieve the level of financial security you desire.

No matter where you are in your career or how much money you make, this seminar will show you how to prepare for a secure financial future.

You will learn the steps you must take to enjoy the benefits of sound money management right now.

WHO SHOULD ATTEND THIS SEMINAR

This seminar is for you if you are interested in finding out how to retire financially independent.

SEMINAR CONTENT

Module I. An Overview on Financial Planning

- What is financial planning
- The investment pyramid
- Asset allocation

Module II. Examine and Diagnose

- Evaluating your financial condition
- Setting your goals
- Steps to success

Module III. Investment and Tax Planning Strategies

- Qualified retirement plans
- Investment vehicles
- Your personal plan

Module IV. Planning for the Future

- College funding
- Retirement planning
- Estate planning

Take Action, Enroll Today! Call (201) 864-9149
Take Control of Your Money and Your Future

Page 2

HERE'S WHAT OTHERS ARE SAYING ABOUT "TAKE CONTROL OF YOUR MONEY"

"Stimulating, provocative, and informative presentation."
Susan Goldstein
V.P., Citibank

"Your program was by far the most important seminar I've attended in a long time. I can't thank you enough."
George J. Wilson
District Manager, IBM

"A program whose time has come."
Richard Zeif
Pres., The Negotiating Institute

"Tremendous learning experience."
Mary Ann DeCarlo
AT&T

IT'S EASY TO REGISTER

- Regular Tuition: $125 per participant

- Super Saver Registration: $99 per participant, when you register 10 days or more in advance.

- ALL MAJOR CREDIT CARDS ACCEPTED

- BY PHONE: Call us now at (201) 864-9149

- BY MAIL:
  Mail registration form to:
  Paul Stuart Associates
  899 Boulevard East, Suite 6A
  Weehawken, N.J. 07087
  Make checks payable to:
  Paul Stuart Associates

Date: September 17.
Place: Holiday Plaza Hotel
West New York, NJ
Time: 9:00 AM–4:00 PM

- - - - - - - - - - - - - - - -

Paul Stuart Associates
899 Boulevard East, Suite 6A
Weehawken, N.J. 07087

Back Cover

Here's How You Will Benefit by Attending This Seminar

- Increase Your Assets
- Reduce Your Taxes
- Successfully Manage Money
- Plan for a Prosperous Retirement

SUPER SAVER REGISTRATION

The regular tuition for this seminar is $125 per person.

To reserve your seat for only $99, simply call and charge your registration to American Express, Mastercard, or Visa at least 14 days prior to the seminar.

Call (201) 864-9149

Your Seminar Leader

PHOTO

Paul Stuart is a Certified Financial Planner. He has 18 years experience helping individuals achieve financial freedom.

What You'll Receive

Take Control of Your Money

Specially Designed Seminar Handbook

Every participant will receive a comprehensive handbook for use during the seminar and afterwards.

It contains all the major points covered during the course of the day, as well as specific action steps you will take to achieve your professional goals.

Personal Financial Fitness Exam

This valuable evaluation process will enable you to define the exact steps you need to achieve total control of your financial future.

Complimentary Consultation

Each and every participant will be entitled to a free one-to-one consultation at the conclusion of the seminar.

This is an ideal opportunity to receive professional guidance and feedback. You will get answers to your specific personal questions.

Save Money . . . Register Early . . . Call (201) 864-9149

Page 3

The Letter Invitation

This a two-piece marketing package consisting of a letter and a reply postcard. The letter describes your event and its benefits and is usually written in a conversational style. Here is an example.

Sample Invitation Letter

YOUR LETTERHEAD

Prospect's Name
Prospect's Address
City, State, Zip

Dear Prospect's Name:

What if you could master the strategies for creating and maintaining more wealth?

I'd like to invite you and (spouse's name, if known) to attend our free "Winning Financial Planning Seminar."

Here's what you'll learn:

• How to substantially reduce your taxes.
• How to guarantee a financially rewarding retirement.
• How to double your CD rates.
• How to protect yourself from inflation's disastrous effects.
• How to safely manage your money for maximum return.

How would your future change if you learned financial planning strategies that will enable you to make informed decisions?

Here's an opportunity for you to learn with *no obligation.* We promise this will be strictly an informational seminar. We will *not* discuss any specific product.

Plan to attend. Call today.

"Winning Financial Planning Seminar"
Date:
Time:
Place:

Seating is limited. Call (telephone number) or mail the enclosed postage-paid card for your RSVP.

This seminar is an educational event. There is no charge.

The Wedding Style Seminar Invitation

This approach is a little more expensive but it is a very effective direct-mail package. It is also a two-piece mailing and consists of an invitation styled like a wedding invitation and a postage-paid return postcard.

Sample "Wedding Style" Seminar Invitation (Front View)

You are cordially invited to be our guest
at a very special financial seminar to be held at

The Exclusive Hotel
899 Fulton Street
Mytown, NY 12701

Hors D'oeuvres and Reception
Wednesday, March 7, 199?
6:30 - 8:30 PM

R.S.V.P.

Sample Wedding Style Seminar Invitation

Winning Financial Planning Seminar

A seminar designed to enable you to create and
maintain more wealth based upon informed decisions.

Here's what you will learn at this seminar:

- How to substantially reduce your taxes
- How to guarantee a financially secure retirement
- How to protect yourself from the effects of inflation
- Investment strategies that double your CD rates
- Safely managing your money for maximum returns

Here's an opportunity for you to learn with no obligation.
We will not discuss any specific products.

Plan to attend. Seating is limited. Make your reservation today.

Please call Marilyn Belle at (419) 833-7453,
or mail the enclosed postage-paid card for your R.S.V.P.

Sample Postage Paid Postcard

☐ **Yes, I will be able to attend your Winning Financial Planning Seminar.**

☐ **No, this date is inconvenient. Please let me know about future seminars.**

Name _____

Telephone number _____

Address _____

City_____ State_____ Zip _____

SHOULD YOU USE A PROFESSIONAL TO DESIGN YOUR MATERIAL?

By following the steps described in this chapter, you will certainly be on target with your marketing material. But if you feel you need more help, there are a variety of professional services available that will produce your brochure and marketing material for you.

Each one of these professionals deals with a wide range of clients. Ideally you want to work with individuals who have had experience in the financial industry. Even if you find some who have, there is a very good chance that none of them have ever helped design marketing materials for a financial seminar. Therefore, you need to supply them with lots of information if you expect them to hit the mark.

Educate them about your audience and your objectives. Describe your TADA to them. Show them similar material you may have gathered from colleagues, and describe the style and approach you like.

Be sure you create a collaborative environment with each of these professionals. Always ask yourself, "Do I feel good working as a team with this person?" Keep in mind that you need someone who can create quality work and is a good personal match for you.

The following describes professionals you can team up with in creating quality marketing materials.

Graphic Designers

Graphic designers will help you create your professional image through your materials. They will get everything ready to go to the printer. They can also help you to choose formats, colors, type fonts, and the type of paper best suited for your needs.

The advent of desktop publishing has spawned innumerable graphic design businesses, the majority of which are one-person shops. Quality and experience can vary greatly between these small designers, but many of them are excellent. Request to see examples of their work and you'll know if they are right for you.

You should also ask colleagues for recommendations, or call your local printers for referrals. Many printers have a graphic designer on staff. If so, you can usually save money by using an in-house graphic designer. Another option is to look in the yellow pages of your phone book under "Graphic Designers" or "Advertising Art, Layout & Production Service."

RESOURCES

The Graphic Artist Guild has a service which can provide you with a graphic artist. If you decide to use this service, allow enough time for them to do a search for you.

Graphic Artist Guild
11 West 20th, 8th Floor
New York, NY 10011
(212) 463-7730
Fax (212) 463-8779

Copywriters

Copywriters will write all the text, or copy, you need for your seminar brochure and marketing material. Once they are clear on your goals, they will write the words that will get the response you want.

The best way to find a freelance copywriter is ask colleagues for recommendations. Graphic designers are also an excellent source for recommendations for copywriters since they usually work hand in hand with them.

RESOURCES

Adweek, a weekly advertising industry magazine contains a number of ads offering freelance copywriting services. They also publish an annual directory, *Adweek*/Art Director's Index USA which contains a listing of freelance copywriters.

Adweek
49 East 21st Street
New York, NY 10010
(212) 995-7323

Advertising Agencies and Public Relations Firms

Although both of these types of companies can help you, they are probably overkill for your small needs. They can design your material, write your copy, and produce it for you, but you will pay a premium for the convenience and it may not translate into higher quality.

You can check the yellow pages under "Advertising Agencies" or "Public Relations," but recommendations are by far the best source for finding an advertising agency or PR firm.

HOW TO FIND THE BEST PRINTER

There are lots of printers you can employ—the problem is that many of these printers are not the best choice for you. You must find the printer who is the right match for you.

Follow these steps and you will secure the best printer in the least amount of time.

1. Interview several printers on the phone. Tell each printer the kind of paper you want, how many colors, and the size

of the print run. Depending on the response, you will quickly find out if you should continue to step two.

2. Show the printer your exact layout. The printer will probably have a few more questions after seeing the job.

3. Ask for a price quote. You are going to want to comparison shop, so make sure each printer is providing a quote on the same job. Ask each printer how long that price will be held, and be sure to get everything in writing.

4. Ask for a delivery schedule. You might be working on a tight schedule. Even if you are not, ask the printer how many days it will take to complete the job. A great price means nothing if you are forced to cancel your seminar when you don't get your brochures in time.

Chapter Eleven

How to Promote
Your Seminar
with Direct Mail

Direct mail is one of the most common and successful methods for promoting financial seminars. It is also a marketing strategy that requires careful study and attention.

RESOURCES

The Direct Marketing Association (DMA) specializes in providing up-to-date information about direct mail and other forms of direct marketing. DMA offers a wide variety of educational resources, newsletters, publications, and conferences that will assist you in learning this type of promotion. For a complete education in direct marketing, DMA is one of the best sources.

Direct Marketing Association
6 East 43rd Street
New York, NY 10017-4646
(212) 768-7277
Fax (212) 599-1268

While you want to receive a high number of registrations from your mailing, it is more important to get qualified and motivated participants to attend your seminar. It is even more important to get a high closing ratio. Therefore, never lose sight of your ultimate objective when making decisions regarding your direct-mail campaign.

HOW TO CHOOSE THE RIGHT MAILING LIST

The mailing list is undoubtedly the most important factor in direct mail. If you have followed the golden rule of TADA, you will have no trouble finding the right mailing list. Response rates from mailing lists can vary from 1/2 of 1 percent to as high as 5 percent.

It is frightening to ask an aspiring financial seminar leader who should attend a seminar and receive the reply, "Everyone!" If this were true, we would have to purchase mighty big mailing lists.

On the other hand, if the aspiring seminar leader replies, "Individuals with an income of $75–100,000, with two or more children under age 7, living within a 20-mile radius," finding a mailing list would be a quite simple.

TADA will define which mailing list is the right mailing list. You can create a TADA with income level, profession, geographic area, age, sex, and so forth. The principle remains the same: define your audience and you've defined your list.

WHERE TO PURCHASE A MAILING LIST

Actually, you don't purchase a mailing list, you rent it. You purchase the labels and the right to do a mailing using the list.

Don't forget this important fact: each list has a number of phony names and addresses. If you attempt to use the labels any more times than you have paid for, you will get caught and could be prosecuted. However, once an individual responds to your mailing, this person is eligible to be placed on your own mailing list. There are two primary sources for mailing lists:

1. *Direct Mail Lists Rates and Data*, the encyclopedia of mailing lists. Its publisher, Standard Rates and Data, has more than 20,000 lists available. This directory allows you to locate almost every conceivable kind of direct-mail list, and can be found in most business libraries. It is published by:

Standard Rates and Data
3004 Glenview Road
Wilmette, IL 60091
(800) 323-4588

American Business Lists is another excellent source for both business lists and households. This company specializes in compiling its own lists from such sources as telephone books, mail surveys, annual reports, and government agencies. Call or write for their free catalog.

American Business Lists
P.O. Box 27347
Omaha, NE 68127
(402) 592-9000
Fax (402) 331-1505

2. List brokers. Instead of spending hours searching for the perfect mailing list, you can go directly to a list broker, who has access to practically every list available. See the yellow pages of your phone book under "mailing lists" to find list brokers in your area.

The list broker functions as a consultant. He or she will work hard to help you achieve your goals, knowing that if you are successful, you will probably come back for more. For the most effective use of a list broker's services, carefully describe your objectives and your TADA.

One of the best things about the list broker is that you don't pay for the service. The broker gets the commission from the list source. You will pay the same charge from the list broker as you would if you purchased the list directly from the source. In fact, sometimes they can negotiate an even better price than you could.

MAILING LIST COMPONENTS

When you purchase mailing lists from a broker or directly from the individual or organization that owns the list, examine and evaluate the list.

The following are the components that describe a mailing list:

1. The source of the list. Some lists are compiled from a variety of sources, some are members of specific organizations, and so forth.

2. Rental rates. Rates can vary widely, from $6 per thousand names to $100 per thousand. The rate depends mainly on the source and how parameters are defined. For example, a list of households by income level would be less expensive than a list of single parent households, above a certain income level, in a specific age group.

3. Minimum purchase. Most list brokers will maintain a minimum purchase amount. In most cases it will be approximately 5,000 names.

4. How often the list is "cleaned" (updated). Because lists deteriorate quickly, make sure any list you rent has been cleaned fairly recently.

5. Kinds of labels available. Practically all labels are available in self-adhesive and cheshire format. Cheshire labels require a machine to apply them. Some labels are now available on computer disk and magnetic tape format.

HOW TO GET THE BEST MAILING LIST

You should always continue to build your own mailing list. Ultimately, this will be your most lucrative list. The return rate on your house mailing list will be two or three times greater than a list you purchase. Be sure to include the following individuals on your mailing list.

1. Referrals and inquiries. Every time someone calls you for information or responds to any form of lead generation program, put them on your mailing list.

2. People who have heard you speak. If you are giving talks at the local rotary clubs or other service clubs, ask for a list of those who attended and put them on your list.

3. No shows. Add anyone who signed up for a seminar and did not attend to your mailing list for future seminars. Many of these individuals will attend a future seminar.

3. Seminar alumni. You will also want to put alumni from your seminars on your mailing list. If they haven't taken advantage of your services, your mailings will remind

them of your availability, or they will pass on your material to others.

4. Current clients. You don't have to mail every seminar notice to your current clients, but keeping them updated on a regular basis is a good idea. It is certainly a good idea to have them on a database, regardless.

HOW TO TEST YOUR DIRECT-MAIL PROGRAM WITH THE A/B SPLIT METHOD

Direct mail can be expensive. You want your mailing to be efficient and attract quality people to your seminars. Therefore, continuous testing should be integrated into your direct mail program.

The fundamental technique for testing in direct mail is called the A/B Split. Here's an example of how to use the A/B Split Testing method.

Let's say you want to evaluate which works better: a wedding style invitation or a letter style invitation.

Step 1. Identify a list that has already gotten good response or a list that is likely to get good response.

Step 2. Ask for the list to be divided in half for an A/B Split Test. This is accomplished by a computer command that will choose all the odd numbered names for one list and the even numbered names for the other. The computer will code one set of labels "A" and the other list "B."

Step 3. The wedding style invitation is mailed to the "A" group and the letter style invitation to the "B" group.

Step 4. Track the results. You can provide one telephone number for "A" group response and another for "B" group response, or you can use a code on the label itself.

The A/B Split allows you to test any element of your direct-mail program and identify the most effective package. There are lots of *theories* about what works best, but the A/B Split provides you with statistical reports on what actually works best.

TEST BEFORE YOU INVEST

Before you roll out your seminar program make sure you are maximizing your returns. The following are the important factors to test:

1. The list. Before you begin to test using the A/B Split, you must test your list. You will want to test your mailing with 1,000 names.

2. Seminar fee or free. Should you charge for your financial seminar? The debate goes on. Test your target audience and find out which works better. Be sure to evaluate the quality of seminar participant.

3. Seminar mailing design and copy. You can test brochure versus invitation style versus letter style. There are lots of design and copy questions that will arise, and they can be decided with a test.

4. Location. This factor can be tested in the same mailing without an A/B Split. Simply list a variety of locations in the same mailing.

5. Day and time. Day and time can also be tested without an A/B Split. List multiple dates and times.

6. Self-mailer versus envelope. Brochures can be folded and mailed without an envelope. In some cases putting the marketing material in an envelope increases response.

7. Bulk mail versus first class. Bulk mail rates cost approximately 45 percent less than first class. The savings can therefore be substantial if you are conducting 10 or 20 seminars a year. However, bulk mail is low priority and can sometimes take weeks to reach its destination.

   There is also the question of perception, since bulk mail is oftentimes viewed as junk mail. You may not want to tarnish your image, especially if your TADA is upper income individuals. Still, you might want to test bulk versus first class mail. You may find it is well worth the savings to use bulk mail. Contact your local post office for a bulk mail permit number.

8. Mail permits or postal meter versus stamps. Using a printed mail permit number, also called an indicia, or

a postal meter, can save you money on the front end, but might substantially reduce your return on investment.

9. Multiple mailings. As a rule, multiple mailings to the same names will increase the response rate. Testing your mailing will determine if this method is a cost-effective strategy for you.

RESOURCES

Target Marketing is a monthly magazine that provides lots of tips specifically about direct mail. If you want to stay current and continue to improve your direct-mail campaigns, this magazine is a good investment.

Target Marketing
401 N. Broad Street
Philadelphia, PA 19108
(215) 238-5300

COST OF DIRECT-MAIL PROMOTION

Of course, the size of your mailing will be the predominant factor in determining your direct-mail cost. Expenses break down as follows:

1. Marketing material. The brochure or marketing material design and printing can be approximately 30 percent to 50 percent of your direct-mail expense. Printing costs vary depending upon paper stock, number of colors, number of components in the direct mail package, and so forth.

2. Postage. Postage is the second most costly expense in direct-mail marketing. Postage will vary according to the type of mail service you use and the weight and size of your package.

3. List rental.

4. Mail house services. There are number of mailing house services that can save you both time and money.

Outsourcing your direct mail will leave you free to handle more important issues. The best way to find a good mailing service near you is to look in the yellow pages under "Addressing and Mailing Services," "Direct Mail," or "Letter Shop Services."

"Seminars Plus" is a convenient and money-saving mailing service that works exclusively with the financial services industry. It is a one-stop service that will provide you with a custom-printed seminar invitation package, a targeted mailing list, and discounted postage programs. Best of all, they do it all. Call for their free sample package.

CIS Marketing, Inc.
612 Corporate Way
Valley Cottage, NY 10989
(800) 825-6900 or (914) 268-5100

CHECKLIST AND TIMELINE FOR YOUR DIRECT-MAIL PROGRAM

The following is a list of tasks and a timing sequence for your initial direct mail program:

Weeks before
program

24   Begin writing and designing the marketing material.

22   Interview graphic designer, copywriter, mailing list supplier, and mailing service, if needed.

20   Select support team.

16   Complete first draft of marketing materials.

14   Complete brochure.

12   Interview and select printer.

7   Mail marketing material, if mailing twice.

4   Mail marketing material.

3   Follow up by telephone, if required.

Chapter Twelve

Filling Your Seminar Seats with Advertisements

CHOOSING THE BEST ADVERTISING MEDIUM

The two most effective advertising media for promoting financial seminars are newspapers and radio. Advertising is an expensive method for attracting participants to your seminar. Therefore, you must constantly improve your response rate. Like direct mail, there are a number of factors that contribute to your response rate and you should test as many elements as possible.

Naturally, TADA plays an important role in selecting the best advertising. Who are you trying to reach? What media do they respond to? What section of the newspaper do they read? What radio station do they listen to?

Choose the section of the newspaper your TADA is most likely to read. In some cases it might be the lifestyle section, while in others it might be the sports section.

If you are conducting seminars locally, you are probably familiar with your local media and which ones are the most appropriate. When in doubt, you can research the demographics of the audiences.

Don't be taken in by low advertising rates. Low rates mean low exposure. As always, you get what you pay for. Ask yourself if your advertising investment is going to bring in the return you're seeking.

RESOURCES

Standard Rates and Data publishes numerous directories that list all newspaper, magazine, radio, and television advertising vehicles. These directories include demographics, advertising rates. and contact names of each outlet. Categories include: Spot Radio Rates and Data, Spot Television Rates and Data, Business Publication Rates and Data, Consumer Magazine Rates and Data, and Newspaper Rates and Data.

Standard Rates and Data
3004 Glenview Road
Wilmette, IL 60091-9970
(800) 323-4588

NINE RULES FOR CREATING A SUCCESSFUL NEWSPAPER AD

Newspaper advertising continues to be the number one media for promoting financial seminars. Many newspapers will help you create an effective advertisement if you let them know basically what you want to say. You can also, of course, create your own ad. Here are some rules to follow when creating a newspaper advertisement.

1. Use a headline. The objective of your headline is to attract the reader. Simple headlines like, "Find out how to substantially reduce your taxes this year," or "Enjoy Your Retirement," or "Learn how to invest in mutual funds," can work quite well.

Don't forget the magic of one of the most loved words in the English language: FREE. Your headline could be as simple as "Free Financial Planning Seminar."

Effective advertising headlines usually offer a reward of some kind. Nothing is more natural in an advertisement for a financial seminar than to offer increased profits, new ways to save money, or anything of the like.

Great idea: Pick up the latest copy of a consumer financial magazine like *Money, Worth,* or *Smart Money.* Check out the titles of the
articles. Nearly every one of them would make a great headline for
your advertisement.

2. Your visual should reinforce the benefits of your seminar. For
example, if you are presenting preretirement seminars, you might
want to show someone enjoying a game of golf. Many people
dream of being able to retire and play lots of golf.

3. The first paragraph of copy should expand the point made
in your headline. For example, if your headline reads, "Reduce
your taxes during the Clinton Administration," you could follow
with copy such as, "Attend a special tax planning workshop that
will enable you to minimize your taxes as a result of current leg-
islation."

4. The layout of the newspaper ad must be visually attractive
to the eye and the copy must be easy to read. The following are
some guidelines for creating a visually attractive and readable ad:

- Keep your visuals simple. Use one primary visual.
- Make the headline as big and bold as the headlines in a
  newspaper.
- Set the body copy beneath the visual and headline.
- Use typefaces that are easy to read. Two of the most popu-
  lar and easy to read typefaces are Helvetica and Times
  Roman.
- Use white space (blank space) liberally so the ad remains
  uncrowded.
- Keep your sentences and your paragraphs short.

5. The advertising copy must describe the benefits of the seminar and the topics that will be discussed. Your copy should be
benefit-oriented—emphasizing saving or making money is the
best technique.

Body copy could read like this:

Why pay more taxes than you have to? The Clinton Administration is providing you with great opportunities to keep more of the money you earn. Attend this seminar and find out how to qualify and what steps you must take.

6. Keep the ad copy as concise as possible. Use only as many words as you need. Edit, edit, and edit again.

7. Keep your copy interesting. You can maintain interest with testimonials and endorsements, by referring to current economic trends, and by offering FREE SEMINAR, FREE LUNCH or FREE DINNER, or FREE WORKBOOK. And don't forget to remind people there will be no obligation to buy anything.

8. Include your photograph. Assuming your ad is not too small, it is a good idea to include your photo and perhaps a one- or two-line bio. People always like to have an idea of who the seminar leader will be. The following is an example of a short bio:

Samantha Choi is a Certified Financial Planner and an active member of the International Association of Financial Planners. She has nine years experience helping others to achieve their financial goals.

9. A call for action. You can ask for the order more than once in the same ad. Ask them to sign up in the headline. Ask them to sign up in the body copy. Ask them to sign up at the bottom of the page. Here are just a few ways to ask for people to sign up for your seminar:

- You are cordially invited to attend . . .
- Announcing a special seminar . . .
- For reservations, please call . . .
- Please reserve my seat at . . .
- Reservations are a must. Call . . .
- Yes, I would like to attend.
- Seating is limited. For reservations please call . . .
- Call today and reserve your seat.
- Attend this special seminar.

RESOURCES

The following books are excellent sources of information for developing your skills and improving your results with advertising.

How to Make Advertising Twice as Effective at Half the Cost, by Herschell Gordon Lewis (Nelson-Hall, Chicago, IL)

How to Write a Good Advertisement, by Victor Schawab (Wilshire Books, North Hollywood, CA)

Tested Advertising Methods, by John Caples (Prentice-Hall, Englewood Cliffs, NJ)

GETTING THE BEST RESPONSE FROM YOUR NEWSPAPER AD

The following guidelines will help you maximize your newspaper ad investment:

1. Sunday is the best day of the week to advertise. A good strategy is to advertise in one Sunday edition and then in one weekday edition a few days before the seminar.
2. The best placement is toward the front of the newspaper or section. You will often pay more for this prime location, but it is worth it.
3. The best location on a page is the upper right hand portion.
4. Multiple exposures will increase your response rate. You can negotiate better responses when you purchase multiple placements.
5. Larger ads attract more response. However, there is a point where your returns will begin to diminish, so test the different sizes and track the response.
6. Save money with regional ads in national publications. Most newspapers like the *Wall Street Journal* offer regional editions with reduced advertising rates.

IS RADIO OR TELEVISION ADVERTISING APPROPRIATE FOR YOU?

At first glance, radio and television advertising can seem very attractive. Your seminar will be promoted to a huge audience and huge numbers of people will show up at your seminar. Right? Not quite.

Broadcast media is tricky for a few reasons. If you purchase a lot of spots in prime time slots, on stations that have a large market share, you will pay heavily. The second problem is that even though you pay heavily, it is still very risky business.

Here is the best strategy for using radio or television to advertise your seminar. If there is a financial or investment talk show in your local area, contact the host of this show. Set up a meeting and arrange a mutually profitable arrangement regarding the individual speaking at your seminar. The host will be interested in talking with you for both the appearance fee as a "celebrity" speaker and for the revenues you will bring in to the radio or television station. You can even make it a sliding scale based upon response. It is important to create a partnership with the speaker. Make sure there is something in it for the speaker if the speaker contributes to the success of the event.

More than likely, the host has a following and his or her appearance as a guest speaker will attract participants to your seminar. (The host might also have a mailing list you can use for your promotional purposes.)

While it is to your benefit to include a well-known speaker in your program, it can also make this promotion technique risky. You may end up attracting individuals who want to meet the celebrity speaker rather than attend your seminar.

When negotiating with a radio or television station, make sure you get everything in writing. A simple letter of agreement stating exactly what the guest speaker will provide, the advertising schedule, the fees you will pay, and any other details you have verbally agreed to will do fine. Your letter of agreement should cover the following points:

- Define the parties involved.
- State the program to be presented.
- Spell out the financial payment to the speaker and the payment schedule.
- State the responsibilities of the speaker, such as reception appearance, and so forth.
- State the time and schedule of the event.
- State your responsibilities.
- Spell out cancellation rights and penalties.

RESOURCES

If you use radio or television advertising on large stations, the calls will come in flurries. There are companies that specialize in receiving multiple phone calls and capturing names and registering people for seminars. Here are two companies that provide these services.

Response Call, Inc.
1785 Cortland Ct., Suite G
Addison, IL 60101
(800) 677-4443

USA 800
P.O. Box 16795
Kansas City, MO 64133
(800) 821-7539

Chapter Thirteen

Increasing Registrations with Free Publicity

The media is looking for you. Yes, it's true. The broadcast media have "dead" air and the print media have blank pages without something to fill the space. You may not make the 6 o'clock news or get interviewed on a national talk show, but there are lots of other opportunities that are easy to access.

BECOME YOUR OWN PRESS AGENT

Free publicity doesn't magically appear—you have to research the available outlets. You must serve the specific needs of the editors and program directors who decide what gets printed or aired and what doesn't.

In this chapter, you will learn the ABCs of publicity, so you don't waste your time or the time of the incredibly busy editors and program directors who will review your material. It's a good idea to start with local print media and talk shows. You will not get any publicity if your only intent is to promote your upcoming seminar; rather, you must have a related "story" to propose. Adhere to the following eight steps and you are certain to meet with success.

EIGHT STEPS TO GETTING MEDIA COVERAGE

Step 1. Match your seminar with the appropriate media. For instance, if your seminar solves financial problems for retired individuals, identify which media is popular with this group. If your seminars are geared toward women, radio shows or magazines geared toward women would be the logical match.

RESOURCES

The following list of directories can help you identify the media that is likely to give you coverage.

The *All-in-One Directory* contains more than 21,000 listings including: daily and weekly newspapers, professional and consumer magazines, and radio and television stations.

All-in-One Directory
Gebbie Press, Inc.
P.O.Box 1000
New Paltz, NY 12561
(914) 255-7560

Bacon's Publicity Checker includes more than 21,000 listings of print media including background information. Bacon's also publishes radio and television directories.

Bacon's Publicity Checker
Bacon's Publishing Company
332 S. Michigan Ave.
Chicago, IL 60604
(312) 922-2400

Radio Contacts lists more than 4,000 radio stations that produce talk shows. The programs and contact person is listed. *Television Contacts* lists more than 1,100 television stations with the same information.

Radio Contacts and *Television Contacts*
BPI Media Services
1515 Broadway
New York, NY 10036
(212) 764-7300

Step 2. Identify the correct person to whom you should send your material. Never send material without confirming the name and spelling of a contact at the station or publication. There is no bigger turn-off to an editor than receiving a letter addressed to "Whom It May Concern" or "Dear Editor."

Step 3.   Use TADA. Customize your material and approach to match the person and media to whom you are sending it. Enclose materials that will connect you to the target audience. For instance, if your seminar is about mortgages, the best place to pitch your story is the real estate section of a major newspaper.

Step 4.   Time your approach. Daily newspapers work on lead times of a week or less. Weekly publications need materials two or three weeks in advance. Sending your material too far in advance is not a good idea, since it might get lost in the shuffle.
Lead time for talk shows can vary. Sometimes they will ask you to be on the show a few days after receiving your material, while other shows will book you weeks or sometimes months in advance.

Step 5.   Mail your press kit.

Step 6.   Follow up with a phone call. Your chances of success will improve vastly if you develop a personal relationship with the decision maker. Your first call can be to confirm that he or she has received the material, and your second call to see if the individual has had a chance to review it, and if so, to discuss it.

Step 7.   Be prepared to discuss your seminar and proposed story. You will most likely be interviewed, so you should be ready with a good sound or video bite. Have a few good stories to tell and even a joke or two that relates to your seminar. Your objective here is to prove that you really are an expert who can help people solve financial problems.

Step 8.   Say thank you. Send a note letting the writer, program director, or host know that you appreciate the opportunity that was given to you.

NINE COMPONENTS OF A PROFESSIONAL MEDIA KIT

If you are seeking free publicity for your seminars, you will need to compose a media kit. The media kit, or press kit, is what you will be presenting to editors and program directors. You will also present it to the decision maker at the various organizations where you'd like to present in-house seminars.

A professional-looking media kit will reward you with huge dividends. You will be chosen first when you are competing with others, because your media kit will reflect your professionalism.

Here are the elements of a media kit and some guidelines for producing or collecting the component.

1. Press Release

The press release is information about your seminar written like a mini news story. The person reading your copy has only a few minutes to decide if their audience would be interested in your information.

That's what "spin" is all about. If you have unique or special information worth sharing, they are likely to give you exposure. The press release has five parts:

1. Contact. This is whom should be contacted for more information or to arrange an interview. Don't forget to include a phone number.
2. Release date. Most press releases are labeled, "FOR IMMEDIATE RELEASE." This means the story can be used immediately.
3. Headline. This is the big and bold statement to get attention and encourage the individual to read on.
4. Dateline. This is the city and state of origin.
5. Body. The body of a press release should no more than four or five paragraphs. Paragraph one gives the who, what, when, where, why, and how. Paragraph two points out the importance of your seminar and the benefits to the target audience. Paragraph three provides information about the seminar, the sponsor, and the seminar leader. Paragraph

four discusses more benefits and reinforces them with a quote. Paragraph five provides registration information.

Follow these rules when writing a press release:

- Double-space your copy.
- Limit it to one page.
- Use short sentences and paragraphs.
- Make sure your grammar and punctuation are perfect.
- Address your press release to a specific individual.
- Avoid hype and edit carefully.

Sample Press Release

FINANCIAL SECURITY ASSOCIATES
123 East Boulevard
Nextexit, NJ 07070
Contact: Rick Maltin
          (201) 265-2338

For Immediate Release

FINANCIAL PLANNING SKILLS EMPOWER WOMEN

Nextexit, NJ—"Money Power for Women" is the focus of a seminar for women who want to take control of their financial future and their lives. It will be held at the Notell Hotel in Fulton, New Jersey, on Wednesday, March 7. This program will begin at 6 PM and end at 9 PM.

In order for women to completely control their own destiny, they must take control of their finances. Diane Keenan, president of the National Association of Women in Business, says, "This program provides women with the skills to achieve fiscal fitness."

Women will learn financial planning strategies and techniques necessary to skills establish credit, reduce taxes, and create an effective plan for retirement. Seminar leader for this program is Marilyn Portnoy, Certified Financial Planner. She specializes in helping women secure their financial future.

This program also helps single and divorced working women solve the unique financial problems they face.

For information or to register, contact Rick Maltin at (201) 265-2338.

2. Cover Letter

A cover letter should be included to reinforce the personal relationship you have established with the decision maker. The primary purpose for writing a cover letter is to make sure your material will be reviewed. Keep it brief and to the point.

The first paragraph should refer to your previous contact or conversation. The second paragraph reinforces the individual's interest in your material. The third paragraph is merely a friendly sign-off.

Sample Cover Letter

FINANCIAL SECURITY ASSOCIATES
123 East Boulevard
Nextexit, NJ 07070

Date
Kharla Garner
KAKE Television
65 Midlan Drive
Washington, NY 12701

Dear Kharla,

It was a pleasure speaking with you today. Thank you for taking the time to discuss the interest and needs of your particular audience.

Enclosed you will find the material you requested, including a copy of an article that was recently published in *Working Woman* magazine. This article provides specific investment strategies for single women.

Kharla, I look forward to the possibility of appearing as a guest on your show.

Sincerely,

Marilyn Portnoy

---

3. Bio

Your bio must answer two very important questions: What makes you qualified to speak on *this* topic? What benefits can you bring to those who will be attending your seminar?

Your bio should not be a resume. It should be narrative in style and interesting to read. A good test for a bio is to read it out loud and see if it flows. Use the following as a guide for how to write your bio and what you should include:

- Limit it to one page, double-spaced.
- Provide information specific to your TADA.
- Refer to the benefits others have received from you.
- Include professional designations and affiliations.
- Give evidence or facts that reinforce your competence.
- Limit your academic history unless it is relevant.

Sample Bio

Bio
Marilyn Portnoy

Marilyn Portnoy has 12 years of experience helping women take control of their financial lives. She is president of Financial Security Associates and as a consultant and seminar leader has helped thousands of women establish their financial goals and achieve them.

She is a Certified Financial Planner and is an active member of the International Association of Financial Planners and the American Seminar Leaders Association.

Recently Marilyn was honored by being chosen to be a member of the Governor's Council for Women in Business. Marilyn believes, "Financial freedom is the final frontier in the journey to empower women."

4. Photograph

You will need a photograph of yourself for media kits and brochures. You don't need to hire a high-fashion photographer, but one who is familiar with executive photography is helpful. The yellow pages of your telephone book will provide you a list of local photographers you can choose from.

The following are some important rules to follow:

- Get black and white and color. Sometimes color will be requested and sometimes black and white will be needed.
- Use a headshot.
- Take a few rolls of shots and show the proof sheets to people you trust for some second opinions.
- Smile. You'll look better.
- Get 100 5" × 7" copies. Printing in quantity is much more cost effective.

RESOURCES

The following photo printing companies are extremely economical. They specialize in printing head shot photographs.

Better Photos Custom Lab, Inc.
525 W. 52nd St., 7th Floor
New York, NY 10019
(212) 757-3988
Fax (212) 974-4655

Ideal Photo
145 West 45th St.
New York, NY 10036-4008
(800) 929-4775 or (212) 575-0303

5. Tearsheets and List of Previous Appearances

As the old adage says, "Nothing succeeds like success." You are more likely to get publicity in the future if you've gotten publicity in the past. As you receive press coverage, collect a list of broadcast media appearances and clean copies of any print publicity, called tearsheets.

6. Articles and Books You've Written

Getting your words into print is still one of the most powerful ways to establish credibility. Invest in professional reprints. Many publications offer their writers reprint services. Also, if you have published a book, always include a copy of it in your press kit.

7. Seminar Brochure

If you have a brochure for your seminar, it should be included in the media kit.

8. Company Brochure

This will provide some background information on your organization.

9. Sample Question List

This is especially important for broadcast media. In many cases the program director arranges the on-air interview, and the sample question list will be what your host works from. The following is an example of a sample questions list:

1. What are the best methods to reduce taxes?
2. Is a savings account the best way to ensure financial security?
3. What is risk tolerance?
4. What is asset allocation?
5. Will the average person be able to retire comfortably?

RESOURCES

The Public Relations Society of America provides a wide range of educational resources for developing your public relations skills.

Public Relations Society of America
33 Irving Place
New York, NY 10003
(212) 995-2230

A GUARANTEED METHOD FOR GETTING ON NATIONAL TALK SHOWS

If you want to land a spot on a national talk show, here is a sure-fire method that is relatively inexpensive. *Radio-TV Interview Report* is a bimonthly magazine that is distributed to more than 4,700 talk show producers and hosts. If you purchase an ad in the magazine, the magazine will help you create an ad will get you the best response. After the ad is published, sit back, answer the phone, and set up appointments to be interviewed on the show.

Radio-TV Interview Report
Bradley Communications Corp.
135 East Plumstead Ave.
Landsdowne, PA 19050-1206
(215) 259-1070

The Yearbook of Experts, Authorities, and Spokespersons is another good method to get national exposure. This directory is sent out to 7,000 of the top journalists in America. Here again there is no guarantee on results, but if you position yourself as an expert on a specific financial topic, there is an excellent chance you'll get a good response.

Mitchell Davis
Broadcast Interview Source
2500 Wisconsin Ave. NW, Suite 930
Washington, DC 20007-4570
(202) 333-4904

HOW TO TURN PUBLICITY INTO PROFITS

If you don't think you're ready to transform publicity into money, it's wise not to waste your time with it. If you decide to appear on talk shows and be interviewed in print articles, the following simple, three-step process will enable you to capture leads that will ultimately result in business for you:

Step 1. Set up an 800 number. You can arrange with Sprint, MCI, or AT&T to set up an incoming 800 number on your regular telephone line.

Step 2. Provide an incentive to respond. Offer a *free* financial tip sheet, a *free* report of some kind, a *free* financial planning guide, or anything free.

Step 3. Stipulate to the media contact you would like the 800 number and free offer mentioned.

The people who respond to your offer are excellent prospects for your seminar, and they are certainly worthwhile additions to your mailing list. If your media exposure is local, some respondents might be good candidates to offer a free consultation.

If your products and services can be marketed on the phone, you can build business on a national level.

THE "MIGHTY MOUSE" METHOD
FOR FREE SEMINAR PROMOTION

One of the easiest ways to fill your seminar seats is to harness the power of the free calendar announcement. Practically every newspaper offers their readership a list of current events, and frequently the listing is free.

First identify newspapers in your area that your target audience is likely to read and find out if they publish a calendar of events. Then find out the contact person and the deadline for placing a calendar announcement. Keep a list of deadlines and mail your announcement in a timely fashion.

After you appear in the calendar once, there is a good chance you will continue to get listed. Like all publicity, you have to follow up and touch base with the contact person regularly. The calendar announcement is an abbreviated version of a press release.

Follow these guidelines for producing your calendar announcement and submitting it:

1. Double-space the copy on your letterhead.
2. Provide a release date.
3. Include a contact name and telephone number.
4. List the who, what, where, when, and why.
5. Include the seminar price.
6. Keep it short—about 50 words.
7. Mail or fax it three or four weeks before the event.
8. Follow up with a phone call.

Sample Calendar Announcement

Financial Security Associates
123 East Boulevard
Nextexit, NJ 07070
Contact: Rick Maltin
          (201) 265-2338

                                        For Immediate Release

Learn investment strategies that will enable you to reduce your taxes, take control your financial future, and plan for your retirement.

"Money Power Seminar" will be held at the Notell Hotel in Fulton, New Jersey, on Wednesday, March 7. Seminar leader for this program will be Marilyn Portnoy, President of Financial Security Associates. This seminar is free.

For more information or to register, call Rick Maltin at (201) 265-2338.

Chapter Fourteen

Using the Telephone to Market Your Seminar

You may have negative associations with telemarketing—many people do. Nonetheless, telemarketing is one of the easiest and most cost-effective techniques for promoting a financial seminar.

ADVANTAGES AND DISADVANTAGES OF TELEPHONE MARKETING

The following lists summarize the advantages and disadvantages of promoting your seminar with the telephone.

Advantages

1. You can work with a relatively short lead time. For example, you can fill the seats of your seminar in two weeks or less.
2. Assuming you will be phoning in a local area, the telephone is a cost-effective approach to marketing your seminar. Your primary expense will be the salary for the telemarketers.
3. The telephone provides you with the opportunity to begin to build rapport with your seminar participants.

Disadvantages

1. You will need to hire, train, and manage the telemarketers or find the right person who can do it for you. If you have never used the telephone to promote or sell, you might have some difficulty with this process.
2. There are logistical challenges. You will need to have at least two—preferably three or four—telephones available. If your office is not equipped or phones are not available, telephone promotion could become too costly.
3. Your target market might be difficult to contact by phone because of their busy schedules. The telephone approach is ideally suited for inviting people within a specific geographical area who can be contacted relatively easily.

HIRING YOUR CALLERS

There are two methods to secure your telemarketers: using a temp agency or finding them yourself. If you can find a temp agency that can provide you with experienced callers, you will certainly be ahead of the game. You will have streamlined your task list. The temp agency will also take care of all the paperwork associated with employees.

If you cannot locate a temp agency, the next best choice is to find a source you can rely on for a steady supply of qualified individuals. A nearby college is an example of a good resource. You can list your needs with the college or on bulletin boards. If you find a few good individuals, there is a good chance you can keep them for a year or more. You can also ask them to recruit their friends or acquaintances.

The method that will consume the most time and may also be the most expensive is placing a help-wanted ad in the local paper. You will need to respond to the calls and interview the candidates, and it is very difficult to judge who will be really effective. With experience, however, you will improve and make fewer hiring mistakes.

There is no perfect ad copy for a help-wanted advertisement. See Chapter 12 for suggestions on creating successful newspaper ads. You may want to try a few different ads and track the number of responses.

Here is some copy you might want to begin with:

Make Big Money on the Telephone. No Selling.
Part-time. Must be positive, energetic, and have
a good phone voice. Call 777-7777. Ask for Stuart.

Plan to pay your callers a base salary plus a commission for each person they recruit for the seminar—perhaps a base salary of $10 per hour plus a $5 commission for each recruit who actually attends the seminar. For each seminar participant who eventually becomes a client or purchases your products or services you can give an added financial bonus to the telemarketer who was responsible for getting the person to the seminar. By using a base salary plus commission for actual attendance at the seminar and an added bonus for individuals who purchase your products or services, you will be encouraging your telemarketers to keep the ultimate objectives in mind.

RESULTS YOU CAN EXPECT

The most exciting part of using telemarketing as a promotional strategy is the predictability of positive results. There is no way of knowing your *exact* results, but you will achieve success. Here is the ultimate success factor regarding telephone marketing of any kind:

The Telephone Marketing Golden Rule

One thing I know and I know it well, the more calls I make the more I sell.

Besides The Telephone Marketing Golden Rule, your results will be determined by the quality of your script and how well you train and manage your telephone people.

If you find a telephone person who is talented, enjoys phone work, and fits into your culture, you might want to offer them the responsibility of interviewing, training, and managing callers and the entire operation.

Assuming you've got an effective script and good callers, you can expect to achieve the following results from your telemarketing efforts:

25–50 calls per hour.

5–10 contacts per hour.

1–3 closes per hour.

Part-time or less experienced callers should work in shifts no more than four hours in length. Unless you hire seasoned professionals, shifts longer than four hours do not work well. Enthusiasm and effectiveness will wane quickly after four hours.

Therefore based upon an average of two closes per hour, you can expect each caller to recruit about eight seminar participants per four-hour calling session. If you have three people calling, you can get about 24 confirmed participants per four-hour calling session.

If your three callers work five nights, you will have 120 confirmations for your seminar. Even if you have a no-show rate of 50 percent, your telephone callers will have filled 60 seats.

THE SCRIPT AND HOW TO MAKE IT WORK

There is no perfect telemarketing script, but the following basic elements must be included: an introduction of yourself and your company, why you are calling, what's in it for them, and a request for action.

Seminar Invitation Script

Hello, (Mr./Ms.) _____. My name is _____.
I'm with _____. I'm calling to invite you
to a free financial seminar called _____. This
seminar will provide you with specific strategies and techniques
that will enable you to:

- Save _____.
- Reduce _____.
- Increase _____.

The seminar is free and we will be serving a complimentary
_____.

Does this sound like a seminar you would be interested in attending?

Would you like us to reserve a seat for you?

*(At this point the individual will either express interest and ask for more
information or clearly state that he or she is not interested. Remember to
impress on the individual you will not be pushing any products.)*

Provide the date, time, and location if the individual has expressed
interest in attending.

(Close by reconfirming their attendance.)

I'll be sending out your seminar confirmation letter today. We look
forward to seeing you on _____, at _____. The
seminar begins at _____ and will end at _____.

A script should never be read—it is merely a format and an outline listing key points the caller must cover during the conversation. Callers should be trained to sound conversational—a warm friendly voice will always achieve better results than a script that is read.

You should also give your callers permission to customize your script. Let the callers adapt the script to their own styles and add or delete words to make the script come alive.

After delivering a script for a few hours, the caller should be able to call without referring to the script. Experienced callers will quickly work from a few notes with some logistical information such as the topic, time, date, and place of the event.

THE BEST TIME TO MAKE CALLS

The best time to make calls to residences is in the early evening. The exact times will vary according to your target audience and geographical location. In general, the best time to phone is between 4 PM and 9 PM on weekdays. Another great time to phone is Sunday evenings during the same hours, when practically everyone is home.

DAILY TRACKING SHEETS

It is essential to keep daily records of each caller. These records will enable you to refine your promotion techniques, improve your efficiency, and evaluate the effectiveness of each caller. The following sample tracking sheet works well.

Using a tracking sheet similar to the sample shown here, have each caller put a hash mark after each call, contact, and commitment. A commitment is when the person who is called says they want to attend and you have sent out an invitation to confirm. Each caller should keep a list of the individuals who have made a commitment to attend.

Sample Tracking Sheet

Caller: _____.
Date: _____.
Hours: _____ to _____.

Calls	Contacts	Commitments

At the seminar you must record the names of the participants who show up and provide an added financial bonus to the caller for each person who actually shows up. In addition you can give a prize to the caller who has the most people show up from their list of people who have made a commitment to show.

FOLLOWING UP TO REDUCE NO-SHOWS

As with any seminar registration, you will want to send out a written confirmation to each registrant and follow up with a reminder call just prior to the seminar to reduce no-shows. Mail your written confirmation the day the individual signs up. (If participants register less than three days before the event, you can eliminate the written confirmation.) Some seminar leaders like to mail an actual ticket—it can add importance to the event and can decrease your no-show count by making the registration seem "official."

CREATING A TELEPHONE SEMINAR MARKETING MACHINE

Ideally, you will be promoting seminars on a regular basis. The advantage of this is that you will build *momentum*. As with any form of marketing, repeat exposure has a snowball effect. You'll be amazed at how an individual can be a no-show three times, finally attend one of your seminars, and eventually become a client. As with any form of sales, you must be willing to ask for the order more than once.

After each seminar, place your no-shows on a list and continue to call to invite them to upcoming seminars. Also mail your schedule of upcoming seminars to no-shows, past participants, and current clients.

Chapter Fifteen

The "Unseminar": An Advanced Seminar Selling Strategy

If you've been in the financial services business for a year or more, there is a profitable seminar selling strategy just for you. It's called the "Unseminar."

The truth is, you can create an extremely successful seminar-selling vehicle with no seminar and no selling. Although you won't be able to invite a large number of people, your closing ratio could be twice as high as any "regular" financial seminar.

WHAT EXACTLY IS AN "UNSEMINAR"?

An unseminar is a relaxed dinner gathering at a fine restaurant and/or exquisite location. Attendance will be limited to 15–20 people.

It is essential that you choose the absolute best, most impressive restaurant in your area. Better yet, find an equally impressive location such as a private club or exclusive country club. It is important that you create an elite atmosphere surrounding this event.

The event should be low-key and friendly. You will present a mini-talk on a financial topic that is of interest to your clients.

You can bring in an outside speaker, if you feel it appropriate. In any case, your focus should be on creating a very special evening.

THE PREREQUISITE IS A CURRENT CLIENT LIST

If you have a client list, even a modest one of 40–50 people, you are ready to conduct an "unseminar."

Review the list and identify your "angels." Angels are clients who really appreciate you and the services you have provided. Angels are vocal supporters who are not afraid of recommending you to others. In fact, anyone who has already recommended you or provided you with referrals should definitely be on your invitation list.

Sample Agenda for an "Unseminar"

6:00–6:30 PM   Reception with Open Bar

6:30–7:30 PM   Dinner

7:30–8:30 PM   Presentation

8:30–9:00 PM   Informal discussion for those who want to continue

WHY THE UNSEMINAR FORMAT WORKS

You will undoubtedly achieve success with this format. It is important to understand why this approach to seminar selling is so effective. There are four reasons. First, you are adhering to an old adage in selling: "Give away something for free." The free offer approach is used in an endless amount of selling situations because it works. This approach also creates a subtle indebtedness. Your guests are much more likely to make an appointment to see you again after sharing a nice meal with you.

Second, you are sharing a *special* event. Free financial seminars are fairly common. Free seminars that include a mediocre lunch or dinner are also fairly common. But your offering of an upscale dinner event is much more attractive.

Third, this more relaxed format is an ideal environment for creating productive relationships. Rapport building is effortless. Your prospects will not be anonymous participants in an anonymous hotel conference room. Instead, they will be breaking bread with you.

Fourth, you will be surrounded by five or 10 happy clients who are endorsing your services. Nothing works better than third-party endorsements. It's one thing for *you* to say you're terrific, but it is far more powerful when *someone else* says you are.

Promoting the Unseminar
Is Relatively Inexpensive

Because of the limited size, your promotion is simple. Just get on the phone and invite your best clients to your program.

Explain how the purpose of your program is two-fold: to provide them with an update on financial matters and to introduce yourself to their friends who might profit from your expertise.

Ask your existing clients to give you the names of the guests who have accepted your invitation. Call each guest personally, introduce yourself, and let them know you are looking forward to meeting them in person. Ask a few general, fact-finding questions that will give you some insight into their specific needs. Mail an attractive confirmation letter soon after you have spoken to them on the phone. Several days before the event, contact them once again to confirm.

Promoting this event costs practically nothing. Your time is the only expense, for you will be saving in direct-mail or advertising expenses. Even at the cost of $50–100 per person for dinner, you will be spending much less than if you were promoting an ordinary financial seminar.

P.S. You can probably find a product wholesaler who would be more than happy to share the promotion expenses in exchange for the opportunity to speak for a few minutes at your event.

Conducting Your Program
Is Simple and Relaxed

The beauty of the unseminar is the simplicity of the format and the ease of orchestrating the evening. Follow these steps to success:

1. Plan to have everyone sitting at the same table, and position yourself at the head.

2. Before the meal is served, ask each of your existing clients to introduce themselves, explain their relationship with you, and let them introduce the guests they've brought along.

3. Next, let the guests say a few words about themselves. Ask them to share a little background on themselves, and why they were interested in attending the program. (Hopefully, it will not be just to enjoy a free meal!) Your job is to keep all comments and introductions related to the topic.

4. After dinner, provide financial insights, current tax developments, investment tips, and so forth. Like any seminar, this will help you to establish yourself as an expert and a valuable resource. Make a few important points and then open up to a question and answer period.

5. As with any seminar, follow-up is the key to success. Call each of your guests and ask them for comments and feedback. This is also an excellent time to learn more about their specific situation and financial needs. Before you hang up, be sure to ask them for an appointment.

SOME IMPORTANT GUIDELINES FOR ACHIEVING OPTIMUM PROFITABILITY

It is easy to forget the seminar premise at a social event such as the unseminar. Therefore it is important to observe the following guidelines:

1. Follow the rules of any well-conducted seminar: Start and finish on time, use audiovisual aids when appropriate, and always stick to your topic.

2. Maintain control. Because of the size and unusual format, personalities can overpower the event. Make sure each of your guests gets a chance to contribute or ask questions.

3. Remember the cardinal rule for successful seminar selling: building relationships and trust will result in new business. This rule should be your guide for your own presentation and behavior.

4. Arrive early. If possible, arrange some less formal meetings before the appointed time for the event to begin. You can use this time to meet with your existing clients or be personally introduced to your client's guests.

5. Keep the tone of the seminar conversational. Don't put yourself into an all-knowing type of role. It will turn people off and reduce your accessibility.

6. Stay late. If the program is scheduled to end at 9 PM, plan to stay until at least 10 PM. More than likely, there will be one or two people who will enjoy your program so much that they will want to continue the discussion after the planned part of the evening is over.

7. Minimize or exclude alcohol consumption. Lots of drinking will dissipate the group's energy and will certainly not help you achieve your objectives. Besides, alcohol will add a considerable expense to your program.

8. Take your time in choosing the perfect site. Choose a restaurant or setting that will allow for some degree of privacy. A location with a private room or area that can be sectioned off is your best bet. Stop by and sample the food before your event. Make sure the menu offers a selection that will cater to a variety of tastes and needs: meat, fish, vegetarian, and so forth.

RECEIVE IMMEDIATE AND LONG-TERM REWARDS

The unseminar is easy, cost-effective, nonthreatening, and can actually be fun to conduct. You simply can't lose. You will be strengthening your relationships and building loyalty with existing clients while you are meeting prequalified prospects for new business. By following the simple format and guidelines outlined, your success is assured.

The unseminar format allows for maximum flexibility; just be prepared to refine and revise your program with current trends and issues as they arise. The best way to win with unseminars is to conduct them on a regular basis. This way, individuals who miss one can take advantage of the next. You will also get new angels as you build your business. You will want to give them all the opportunity to attend an unseminar.

Above all else, continue to communicate your sincere concern for the people who attend your programs. People don't care how much you know unless they know how much you care.

Chapter Sixteen

How to Tap the Corporate Market with Seminar Selling

More and more corporations are relying on financial industry professionals to provide financial advice and support to their employees. As more employees take their financial future into their own hands, corporations and businesses will be relieved of the responsibility to provide support.

Seminar selling offers the unique opportunity to position yourself and your services in this fertile market and increase your base substantially. Seminar selling in corporations is a lot like hunting at a zoo. It is difficult, if not impossible, to miss.

TADA: THE MAGIC MARKETING STRATEGY

Let's face it, positioning yourself in the corporate market will require even more decisions. Naturally, your business plan is based upon TADA.

What works for blue collar workers will probably not work for senior level executives. Similarly, what works for men probably won't work for women. Every successful marketing plan requires a clearly defined target audience. Base all of your decisions on TADA, and your decisions will be good ones.

To be successful when marketing your seminar to corporations, you will need a variety of scripts, brochures or marketing materials, and a tracking system. Above all else, you will need patience and persistence to work your way through the corporate maze. But take heart: when you score, you score big.

In many cases, persistence is more important than intelligence. So don't give up. When the administrative assistant puts you on hold for five minutes at a time or disconnects you, don't take it personally. Keep moving, and never give up. If your contact fails to return a call, it's your responsibility to get back to him or her in a timely fashion.

One of the most frustrating aspects of marketing your financial seminar to corporations is the uniqueness of each one. Decision makers and procedures vary from one organization to the next. You might need to speak to the personnel department in one organization and human resources in the next. In a smaller company, the chief financial officer could be the decision maker. Your objective, then, is to identify the key contact person. Often the employee benefits department is a good place to start or will probably be helpful in pointing you in the right direction.

THE WINNING STRATEGY PMP: PHONE–MAIL–PHONE

Phone–mail–phone is the most successful approach for marketing financial seminars to the corporate market. It's back to the basics when you get on the telephone to market your seminar. Scripts are an integral part of the process. There is no substitute for an effective script, which should be customized to your TADA.

Regardless of to whom you are speaking, make sure you convey the message that you have no intention of hard-selling financial products. Instead, tell your prospects you intend to educate, inform, and assist employees in making successful financial decisions. You must constantly focus on gaining the trust of each person you come in contact with and let them know that your intentions are good.

Below is a sample of a good entry script.

Entry Script

"Hi, my name is _____ , I'm with
_____. I'd like to speak with whomever is charge of providing employees of <u>(company name)</u> with personal financial planning information."

It is very likely you will be connected to the incorrect person the first time. So, introduce yourself again and confirm you are speaking to the right person.

"Are you the person who is in charge of providing employees with personal financial planning information?"

You will probably have to provide more information about "what you are selling." Prepare a short description of your seminar and describe a benefit. For example, you might say,

"I'd like the opportunity to provide information that will help members of your company take control of their financial future. We will provide a educational program that will help them achieve that goal."

When you are sure you are speaking to a qualified decision maker and you have identified yourself, you will need to use a script to further qualify your prospect. Your script might continue as follows.

Script to Qualify

"Are you currently providing educational programs that will help your (managers, technicians, engineers, and so forth) achieve their financial goals?

If they answer "yes":

"Are you satisfied with them?"

"What don't you like?"

"How would you like to change them if you could?"

If they are not satisfied with the programs they currently offer, find out what their needs are and try to offer them a program that will fit them. If they answer "no":

"Would you like to provide an educational program that would give your employees the opportunity to learn more about securing their financial future?"

"What steps do I have to take to be considered to present my program at _____?"

At this point they will describe the procedures and possible opportunities for you to present your seminar. For example, they might say, "We do offer lunchtime seminars; send in your material for me to review." They will most likely ask you to mail in your material. Confirm your next step.

"I am going to mail you some background material on my organization, myself, and our seminar program, _____. I must emphasize, I will not hard-sell our financial products and services. But I would like to make my services available to those who would like more assistance."

PRESENTING YOUR MATERIAL

As always, your credibility will be determined by your promotional material. If your organization has seminar promotion material available, take advantage of it. Whenever possible, customize the promotional material for your TADA.

Your material must convey to the decision maker you are familiar with the corporation and the problems and concerns of their employees. It is equally important to communicate that you can provide them with valuable solutions.

As one very successful financial planner says, "It's not what I know, it's how I look." This is especially true when it comes to the quality of the promotional materials for your seminar. In most cases, your material will be glanced over rather than read. Judgments will be made according to the appearance of your materials, so don't short-change yourself and sabotage your efforts. Invest the time and energy in your materials necessary to make them effective.

Here is a checklist for your promotional package for marketing your seminar to corporations.

- [ ] Cover letter
- [ ] Seminar brochure
- [ ] Company brochure
- [ ] Client list
- [ ] Endorsements
- [ ] Seminar materials
- [ ] Articles or books you've written
- [ ] Promotional video

Let's examine each of these items in more detail.

Cover Letter

Your promotional package must always have a cover letter. It will remind the decision maker of your conversation.

Keep your cover letter short. You want the individual to spend time reviewing your material, not reading the cover letter.

Sample Cover Letter for Promoting Your Corporate Seminar

YOUR LETTERHEAD

Dear Bill,

Thank you for your interest in our financial seminar, "Successful Financial Strategies." As I mentioned to you on the phone, we will provide a comprehensive financial planning seminar that will enable your employees to make educated decisions.

Enclosed you will find the material you requested.

Bill, I look forward to speaking with you after you've reviewed our material. We look forward to the possibility of serving you and your organization.

Sincerely,

Paul Stuart

Seminar Brochure and Company Brochure

You will need a seminar brochure as opposed to the invitation you would use in direct mail. Your seminar brochure should be designed along the guidelines outlined in Chapter 10. If your company has a brochure, it should be included (as long as it is not overly sales-oriented).

Client List and Endorsements

Even if your brochure already includes a client list, you can include a more elaborate list on a separate sheet. This will, once again, strengthen your credibility.

It is also essential that you collect endorsement letters from people who have experienced your program. Getting an endorsement letter requires two steps: do a good job and then ask for a letter.

Always ask the decision maker who was responsible for bringing you into the company for an endorsement letter. This person will have most likely collected evaluations and/or has sat in on your program. The letter should be on corporate stationery and should attest to the fact that you provided a good financial seminar to the organization. A good way to facilitate an endorsement letter is to say, "I know you're very busy. If you like I will write one and you can modify it in any way you see fit." Most busy executives will be grateful for your offer and take advantage of it. Some amend your letter and make it even better.

> Great idea: Every time you get an endorsement letter, "white-out" the date. This will make your endorsement letters timeless. Then make 100 clean copies for future use.

Seminar Materials

Include any sample workbooks, books, copies of your slides or overheads, financial health quizzes, and checklists that you may use in a seminar in your package.

If you will be handing out an evaluation form that offers participants the opportunity for a free consultation, include that as well. This will help gain the trust of the decision maker that you are not going to do any hard sell.

Include copies of any articles or books you have written. If you have one, include a promotional video that describes your seminar.

PHONE TO FOLLOW-UP

After you have mailed your material to the decision maker follow up with a call a week to 10 days after you've mailed it. The following is an effective script to use.

Follow-Up Script

"Hi, _____, this is _____ with
_____.
I was just calling to find out if you received the material I mailed
you and to see if you had a chance to review it."

If no:

"When would be the best time to get back to you?"

If yes:

"Does this program look like something that could serve the
employees of _____?"

If yes:

"Where do we go from here?"

*The decision maker will lay out the procedures. It might have to go to the
next higher level or to a committee. After you are clear on the next step,
say,*

"So, when should I check in with you again?"

*You should not accept a vague time; instead, pinpoint a specific date that
will be appropriate for you to call back. Otherwise, you might be directed
to another individual, in which case the process will start over again.
Make sure you confirm your next step.*

"Great! If I don't hear from you by _____, I'll call
you back on _____."

If there is interest, you should set up a face-to-face appointment. Although meeting with a corporate representative will take
up the better part of a day, you will improve your chances of success if you do. A meeting will help alleviate fear and build trust.

ORGANIZE YOUR LEADS

Research shows that the most important strategy for promoting corporate seminars is consistent follow-through.

After you have qualified a corporation and have mailed them your material, you must use a contact system that will guarantee no leads will "fall through the cracks." You can take advantage of one of the many sales software programs available, or use a simple tickler file. But you *must* use something.

Let's say you make a commitment to conduct seminars within corporations and set a goal of three or four seminars a month. In order to achieve your goal, you must generate 50 or 60 qualified leads. It will be impossible for you to follow up properly without a contact system.

The most simple and inexpensive way to ensure a timely follow-up is to place each lead on a 5" × 8" card. Get a file box with two sets of index tabs: one set numbered 1–31, and the second set labeled January to December.

After the initial mailing, you will put the card 10 days ahead. In many cases, however, you will be asked to call the decision maker back in a few months. You would then move the card ahead to the appropriate month. On the first business day of each month you will begin calling the cards that have been placed in that month. Using this system, you can stay on top of the most critical component for marketing your financial seminar to corporations: the follow-up.

If you want to be successful conducting seminars to corporations, you must segregate your seminar selling program from your other marketing efforts. This tickler system will accomplish that need.

RESOURCES

There are many companies that produce sales contact software. Two of the most well-designed products are Act and Telemagic. The best product specifically designed for the financial business is The Bill Good Marketing System.

Telemagic, Inc.
5928 Pascal Ct.
Carlsbad, CA 92008
(800) 835-MAGIC

The Bill Good Marketing System
P.O. Box 1959
Sandy, UT 84091-1959
(800) 678-1480

Act, Contact Software International
1840 Hutton #200
Carrolton, TX 75006
(800) 365-0606

FOR FREE OR FEE?

Building your client base and selling your products and services is your mission. The fees you earn as a seminar leader will be a fraction of what you will earn as a financial consultant.

But there is one excellent reason why you should charge a fee to present your program. It will help dismiss the fear that your seminar is nothing more than a sales pitch. You will be placing value on the presentation itself. You need not ask for a high fee, but do ask. Corporations will have little resistance paying a fee if they believe your program is worth it.

Also, if your handouts are particularly sophisticated, you might want to charge a fee for each workbook.

When Willie Sutton was asked why he robbed banks, he replied, "Because that's where the money is." If you want an affluent client base (and who doesn't?), you should go to the corporations and executive market. Seminar selling continues to be one of the best strategies to penetrate this market.

Persistence and determination are alone supreme! Many of the top producers in the financial industry invest their time and energy delivering seminars to members of this target audience, and you should too. Apply these marketing strategies and you will secure the opportunity to conduct financial seminars in the corporate market.

Chapter Seventeen

How to Capitalize on the In-House Seminar Market

C orporations are just one example of a sponsored program. The opportunities to present sponsored or in-house seminars are practically unlimited. Other organizations that can provide you with the opportunity to present your program to their group include: professional and trade associations, adult and continuing education organizations, service clubs, and religious organizations.

GET PAID TO SELL YOUR SERVICES

The biggest advantage of presenting in-house seminars is the money you will save in marketing expenses. As discussed earlier, you will probably even receive a fee for your program. All continuing and adult education programs charge the public and will offer you a fee, and many trade and professional associations offer honorariums for presenting a program on the regional or national level. Even many religious organizations often offer some form of compensation for presenting your program.

Below is a sample letter of agreement you can use when you are booked to present your seminar in-house.

Sample Letter of Agreement

(Your Letterhead)

LETTER OF AGREEMENT
Between
Your Company and XYZ Company

Dear _____:

Subject: Safe Money Seminar

(Your name) will speak to your group on (Date). The location will be (Hotel or meeting facility) in (City), (State).

This presentation will be _____ in length. It will begin at _____ and end at _____.

The fee for this presentation will be _____ plus expenses, which include roundtrip air fare from (Airport) in (City, state); hotel; meals; and ground transportation.

You will receive one master copy of the handout material, which will be tailored to your organization's program. This will be mailed 30 days prior to the program date. This master copy will then be reproduced by you in sufficient number for each participant to receive one copy.

No tape recorder, audio or visual, may be used without the expressed, prior written permission of XYZ Company.

Upon receipt of a 10 percent deposit of _____ and this signed letter, the proposed date will be reserved for you.

The balance of _____ will be given to XYZ Company prior to the presentation. All expenses will be billed.

Your Company	XYZ Company
By: _____ Pres.	By: _____

TRADE AND PROFESSIONAL ASSOCIATIONS

There are approximately 9,000 trade and professional associations in the United States. Practically all of them hold local, regional, and national meetings. Almost every adult in America belongs to at least one association, if not a few.

Associations need seminar leaders to provide educational programs for their members and they are almost always open to suggestions. Here again TADA becomes your passport to success.
When your materials are customized to a specific target audience,
your chances of success are heightened.

The best way to choose which associations to pitch is talk to
your existing clients. Ask clients what professional organizations
they belong to. Some of these organizations are industry-specific,
while others are job-specific. For example, there are bank associations that mangers belong to and there are management associations that bankers belong to. Figure out where your expertise lies
and approach the associations you feel could benefit most from
your seminar.

Some associations operate only on a national level, while others hold local meetings in a particular region, state, county, or city.
If you want to explore the whole world of associations, examine
any one of these three resources.

RESOURCES

National Trade and Professional Associations of America lists more
than 6,300 associations. It includes background information and
when and where their annual meetings will be held.

National Trade and Professional Associations of America
Columbia Books, Inc.
1212 New York Ave., NW, Suite 330
Washington, DC 20005
(202) 898-0662

Encyclopedia of Associations is a three-volume set and it includes
contact names.

Encyclopedia of Associations
Gale Research Company
Book Tower
Detroit MI 48226
(313) 961-2242

The *Who's Who* of *Association Management* will provide you with the specific contacts on a regional level and the names of individuals who are in charge of educational programming.

Who's Who of *Association Management*
American Society of Association Executives
1575 Eye St., NW
Washington, DC 20005
(202) 626-ASAE

ADULT AND CONTINUING EDUCATION ORGANIZATIONS

Practically every college and university in America offers some form of noncredit continuing education programs. These same types of programming are offered by high schools, libraries, organizations like YMCA and YMHA, and even park and recreational facilities.

In addition, there are thousands of adult education organizations that offer courses in everything from flower arranging to sushi making. These organizations are great opportunities for you to present your financial seminar.

Start by identifying the organizations that offer adult and continuing education programs in your area and call or write for their catalogs. Evaluate each organization's current curriculum and identify a portioning for your seminar. Then follow the marketing steps outlined in this chapter.

> Great idea: If you are presenting your program at a college or university, ask the institution for a camera-ready copy of their logo and print it on your brochure. This will lend credibility to your seminar and increase registration.

SERVICE CLUBS AND FRATERNAL ORGANIZATIONS

Many service clubs and fraternal organizations such as Rotary, Kiwanis, Elks, and Lions clubs need speakers. They are looking for individuals who can deliver a short presentation at luncheon, dinner, and evening meetings.

You must be able to deliver a lively talk that contains relevant information to that specific group. These organizations could be ideal for you if their members fit your TADA.

CHURCH AND RELIGIOUS ORGANIZATIONS

Most church and religious organizations offer a variety of personal development programs. They have a sincere commitment to improving all aspects of the lives of their members.

Your ideal starting point is with your own religious affiliation. Once you've done a good job for one group, collect endorsements and you'll be able to book lots of these in-house seminars. You can then expand to a whole "circuit."

MARKETING STRATEGIES
FOR IN-HOUSE SEMINARS

Marketing your financial seminar to organizations is very similar to marketing to corporations. The Phone–Mail–Phone System will work.

1. Phone: Follow this script when you make your initial call.

Script for Qualifying Decision Maker

I'd like to speak to whomever is in charge of choosing seminar leaders for your _____. Who would that be?

Script for Identifying In-House Booking Procedure

Hi, my name is _____, my company is _____.
I'm calling to find out what I have to do to be considered to present my program, (program title), at your (church, association, club, etc.).

---

2. Mail: Mail the promotional materials described in Chapter 15.

3. Phone: Follow-up is the essential element to getting the booking. Many of the decision makers you will be speaking with in nonprofit organizations and trade and professional associations are volunteers. Booking the seminars for their meetings and programs is not a top priority. Although you will be performing a service for them by phoning them, you will often have to remind them.

Here's another very important detail you should always keep in mind when you are marketing your seminar to organizations. *They need you.* They need speakers and presenters. So keep persevering.

HOW TO GET BOOKED
BY SPEAKERS BUREAUS

The purpose of speakers bureaus is to provide organizations with presenters. There are several different types of bureaus. Some specialize in celebrity speakers who charge $20,000 or $30,000, while others specialize in speakers who charge only $1,000. Bureaus work on a commission basis; commissions generally vary somewhere between 20 percent and 30 percent.

Speakers bureaus will save you time and energy in marketing your program, and they have ongoing relationships with the decision makers at the various organizations.

The Financial Seminar Leaders Resource Guide in the back of this book lists hundreds of speakers bureaus. You can begin by calling and establishing a relationships with the ones you are interested in. Each bureau will explain what they need from you. Many bureaus have data banks where they will list your information. When a suitable opportunity arises, they will call you.

Ideally, the in-house seminar market should be part of your overall seminar selling strategy. Identify the groups that include your TADA and maintain a consistent level of exposure with your TADA by presenting in-house programs.

Some financial organizations retain individuals who do nothing else but market in-house programs. Credibility is immediately established when your program is sponsored in one form or another by an organization.

Chapter Eighteen

Arranging Your Seminar Room for Success

Temperature, lighting, and seating are the three principle elements that can have an extremely negative impact on your seminar if you fail to take complete control of them.

SEMINAR ROOM TEMPERATURE

Always remember the Law of Seminar Room Temperature. Keeping this in mind, it is important to realize that you're probably never going to satisfy everyone.

Law of Seminar Room Temperature

At any given moment during your seminar, half the people in the room will feel it is too warm and half the people will feel it is too cool.

The following are a few tips that will keep complaints to a minimum:

1. When you first arrive, locate the thermostat. Familiarize yourself with the control system. Make sure the temperature is set at a comfortable 68 to 72 degrees.

2. If you can not adjust the temperature, find out who can. Write down the extension number of this individual and make sure this person will be available during the time you will be conducting your seminar. (If you are in a hotel,

the banquet manager will probably be the one responsible.)
If this person is not available, find out who the alternate is.

3. It is always better to keep the room slightly cool rather
   than slightly warm. A warm room makes your audience
   drowsy and less attentive, and it's easy to get warmer by
   putting on additional clothes.

4. Unless the majority of the room feels it is either too hot or
   too cold, refrain from adjusting the temperature.

SEMINAR ROOM LIGHTING

Room lighting is usually overlooked by amateur presenters, but
it will affect both the way your audience feels about themselves
and about you and your presentation. Here are some guidelines
to follow:

1. Arrive early enough to have time to adjust the lighting.

2. Think of yourself as an entertainer when on stage. Make
   sure adjustable lights are focused on where you will be
   standing, just like spotlights.

3. In general, keep the room bright. Find out where the room
   controls are located and make sure the adjustable switches
   are set for maximum brightness.

4. If you will be using a projection screen, turn out any lights
   that are shining directly on the screen. If you can't do this
   without making the room considerably darker, unscrew the
   light bulbs that are nearest to the screen.

5. If you have the luxury of allowing sunlight to shine in, by
   all means take advantage of it. Natural light beats artificial
   light in almost every respect.

SEMINAR ROOM SEATING

Seating arrangements should be considered carefully before any
professional presentation. In ordinary selling, the competent

salesperson carefully positions the body and establishes ideal eye contact. Equal care must be taken in the seminar selling situation.

Do not put your chances for success in the hands of individuals who have no idea what your objectives are. There are two seating arrangement possibilities: what they will give you and what you should ask for.

It is important to learn how to be creative and make adjustments to the standard seating arrangements depending on room size, shape, lighting, lines of sight, and so forth. Let's look at the guidelines and rationale for adjusting seating arrangements and then the primary variations.

1. Always submit a detailed drawing of your seating arrangements to the meeting facility. There is no substitute for a picture of exactly what you want. Rarely will you get exactly what you ask for, but you have a much better chance of getting close to what you want when you submit a drawing.

2. See the room from the eyes of the audience. Sit around the room in various locations and test for comfort. Do you have to crane your neck or twist your body to face the presenter?

3. Move every seat so that it is focused on the presenter. Get creative. Don't limit your seating to straight rows. Straight rows force your audience to focus on blank walls and the backs of people's heads.

4. Avoid placing aisles down the middle. The center of the room is the prime viewing area. Why waste it on an aisle? You can create aisles down the sides or off center and keep the center reserved for what's most important—your audience.

5. Prepare the room with 10 percent fewer chairs than you have reservations. By setting up the room for fewer people than have signed up, two situations can occur. Based on average no-show statistics, you will have the correct number of chairs. However, if everyone *does* show, you will have to arrange for chairs to be brought in at the last moment. This will give your participants the impression that lots of people want to attend your seminar. In either case, the result is best for you.

6. Arrange the chairs as close to you as possible. Remember, you are creating relationships, not just selling. You want to be close to your audience. Many times you can simply move the last row of chairs to the front of the room.

7. Give people enough room to feel comfortable. Assuming your room is big enough, provide instructions to allow 8 to 12 inches between each chair. Your audience will appreciate the additional elbow room.

8. Be prepared to move chairs. Get to your seminar location early enough to rearrange your room exactly the way you want it. After a while, you will identify small modifications that will make a big difference to you.

9. If the room is rectangular, place the chairs along the long side. You will keep the audience closer to you and they will see your visuals more clearly.

The standard seating arrangements for financial seminars are classroom, theater, and banquet style. These are variations based upon the above guidelines. These simple modifications can have a substantial impact on the success of your seminar.

Classroom style. This is often the preferred seating arrangement for financial seminars, because you will be providing tables for holding materials or for doing calculations and writing. Usually these tables are six or eight feet in length, which means two to four seats per table. See Figure 18–1.

Although classroom style provides convenient desk space, it has a few drawbacks. If you have a group of more than 100 people, you will require a large room to accommodate the tables. Large groups set up in the classroom style can create enormous distance between you and most members of your audience. Classroom style makes your interaction with the audience a bit more difficult.

Classroom style variations. Set up your tables in a chevron. This simple modification will allow the members of your audience to have a better view of each other and a better view of you. See Figures 18–2 and 18–3.

FIGURE 18–1
Classroom Style: What They Will Give You

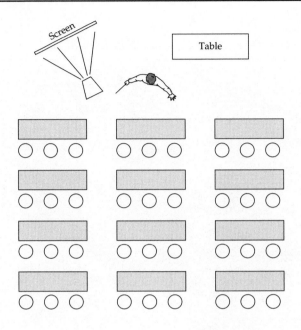

FIGURE 18–2
Classroom Style (Variation 1): What You Should Ask For

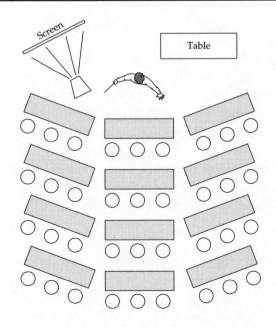

FIGURE 18–3
Classroom Style (Variation 2): What You Should Ask For

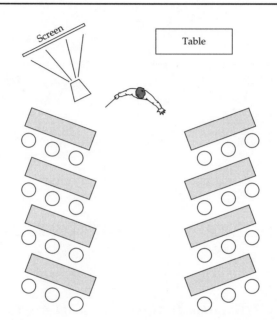

Theater style. Theater style is the most basic arrangement. Chairs are set up in rows. Theater style accommodates a large audience the easiest and allows for good viewing. The disadvantage of theater style is that participants will have no writing surface. See Figure 18–4.

Theater style variation. Set up your chairs in a semicircle and eliminate the center aisle. This will provide everyone with more prime viewing area. See Figure 18–5.

FIGURE 18–4
Theater Style: What They Will Give You

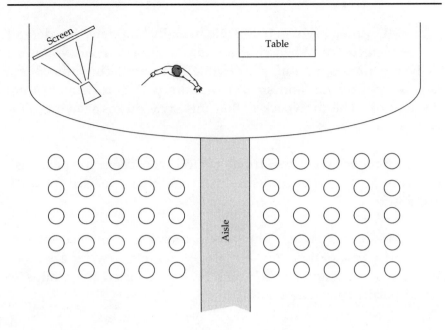

FIGURE 18–5
Theater Style Variation: What You Should Ask For

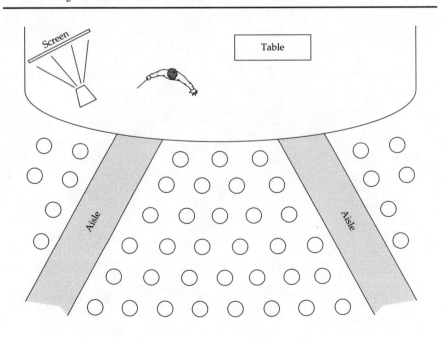

Banquet style. This style usually happens by default rather than choice. When your seminar includes a meal, you must deliver your program after everyone has eaten. The atmosphere is usually convivial and small tables are perfect for small group discussions. The drawback is that this style makes viewing difficult. See Figure 18–6.

Banquet style variation. Before you begin to speak, ask everyone if they would please turn their chairs to face forward. See Figure 18–7.

U-shaped style. This set-up promotes audience interaction and participation. You are also providing a writing surface for your participants. This works best when used for groups of 15–25 participants. See Figure 18–8.

FIGURE 18–6
Banquet Style: What They Will Give You

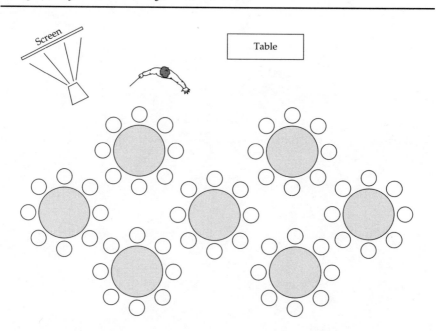

FIGURE 18–7
Banquet Style Variation: What You Should Ask For

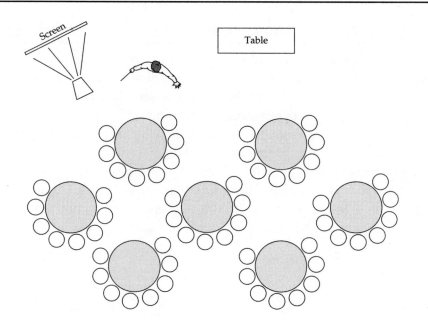

FIGURE 18–8
U-Shaped Style

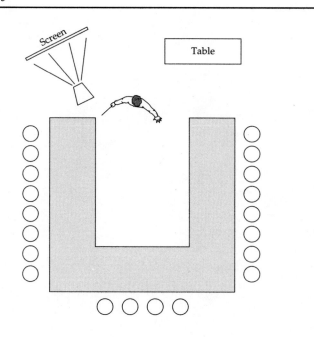

REGISTRATION TABLE

If you are expecting a large group, set up your registration table just outside of the door. This will keep disturbances by latecomers to a minimum. When the group is smaller, the registration table can be placed in the back of the room. Always set up a table in the back of the room for administrative purposes and to place extra handouts, any literature, or other materials.

By taking control of your environment, you will maximize your effectiveness. Financial seminars are most successful when you know how to work them. You're audience will appreciate your professionalism and your profits will be substantially increased.

Chapter Nineteen

The Secrets of the World's Greatest Seminar Leaders

Delivering a dynamic seminar is an art and a science. This chapter discusses a variety of elements that will contribute to your power and success as a presenter.

THE ESSENTIAL ELEMENTS OF PERSONAL PRESENTATION SKILLS

A recent research study led by Professor Albert Mehrabian at the University of Southern California defined the three essential components of personal presentation: visual, vocal, and verbal.

Visual delivery means how you look when you speak. Vocal delivery means how you sound when you speak. Verbal refers to the words you use.

The results of this study showed that the effectiveness of a speaker is determined 55 percent by the visual component, 38 percent by the vocal component, and only 7 percent by the verbal component. (See Figure 19–1.) Your success as a presenter, therefore, will be determined not so much by *what* you say but by *how* you say it.

To maximize your power as a seminar leader, study the elements of each of the following components.

1. **Visual Delivery.** Your visual delivery will be determined by seven elements: your clothing and accessories, groom-

FIGURE 19–1
Components of Personal Presentation

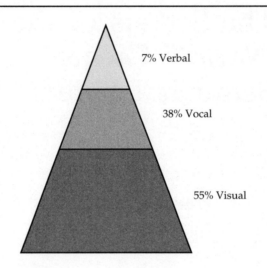

7% Verbal

38% Vocal

55% Visual

ing, facial expression, eye contact, gestures, posture, and movement.

The following are some guidelines for each of these elements.

a. Clothing and accessories. The dress code for financial seminars is classic business attire. The best choice for men remains a white shirt and conservative dark gray or navy blue suit. Stripes of any kind on suits should be avoided. Flair can be added with a colorful tie. It is important to keep all suits well-pressed and to discard any shirt with a frayed collar.

   Although conservative business attire is also the rule for women, there has been slightly more latitude as far as color choices and styles in recent years.

b. Grooming. As a seminar leader, your grooming needs a little more attention than normal. It is always a good idea to take one final look in the mirror before stepping in front of a group to make sure your hair is combed well, your face clean shaven, or your make-up properly applied.

    c. Facial expression. The best facial expression you can possibly wear is a smile. A smile attracts people to look at you and communicates to your audience, "I'm glad you're here," and "I'm glad I'm here."

    d. Eye contact. Eye contact with your audience helps you establish rapport and builds trust.

    e. Gestures. Use gestures to emphasize your points. They make you visually interesting and exciting to watch and listen to.

    f. Posture. Stand tall with your shoulders up and your feet approximately 18 inches apart.

    g. Movement. Try not to spend the entire seminar standing behind a lectern. Get in the habit of moving freely around the room.

2. **Vocal Delivery.** Your vocal delivery will be determined by four elements: tone, speed, volume, and clarity.

    a. Tone. It is essential that you speak with enthusiasm. Nobody is going to get excited about your ideas or presentation unless you do. Use the tone of your voice to emphasize points and add drama to your seminar.

    b. Speed. Be careful not to talk too slowly. Studies have shown people lose interest and have their minds wander if the speaker speaks slowly. This is because the human mind thinks at approximately 750 words per minute, but we speak at only about 250 words per minute. Try to vary the speed of your delivery throughout your presentation.

    c. Volume. Make sure you speak loudly enough. Use a microphone whenever possible, but especially when the room is large or the group is larger than 50 people.

3. **Verbal.** Even though the words you use are responsible for only 7 percent of your impact on your audience, you should choose them carefully. The words you use as a seminar leader can either attract business or repel it. Your words also establish credibility. They provide the logical reasons and emotional foundation for people to want to do business with you.

Avoid using technical financial terminology. You will lose your audience. When in doubt, ask your audience if they are familiar with a term or expression you are using.

Caution: Be extremely careful with your words. Sexist, discriminatory, or offensive language will destroy any chances of winning over your audience. Words that are commonly used in conversation can take on a completely different meaning when used in a seminar setting.

Make sure you say "he or she" as opposed to assuming a gender. For example, if you are referring to a single parent make sure you say, "he or she;" don't assume the female gender. If you fear making one of these gender slips, you might want to say, "I apologize to you in advance if I fail to say "he or she" in every case. It is a mistake. I support equality in all forms." By saying this, you will take yourself off the hook.

WHAT IS THE BEST PRESENTATION STYLE?

You must match your personal delivery style to the particular group you are addressing. Be flexible and willing to adjust your presentation style.

The Best Delivery Style

The best presentation style is a versatile one.

For example, if your audience is the mature market, use a style that is more like theirs. Use humor, expressions, language, references, examples, and case studies that the mature audience can relate to and that reflects their values. Remember, people like people who are like themselves.

YOUR PRIMARY OBJECTIVE AS A PRESENTER

Your primary objective as a presenter is to inspire your audience to action. Great seminar leaders exhibit a motivational quality. Not everyone will decide they will want to continue their relationship with you, but you can improve your closing ratio dramatically by adopting a motivational flavor.

Let's face it, there are many things that you know are good for you, but you don't exactly rush out to do them. People hesitate taking action on everything from getting annual medical check-ups to writing their wills. This is really no different.

But you need to make people to take action. If you continually refer to the benefits of your information and how it will positively impact the lives of your audience, you will motivate them. Your words should continually refer to action. "If you do this . . ." or "If you fail to do this, then . . ." are important phrases that empha-size the benefits of taking action. Your visual, vocal, and verbal delivery must all communicate, "Pay attention. This is important stuff. What I'm telling you will improve your financial future."

Finally, never be self-promotional in what you are saying, because it will almost surely work against you. It is not necessary to tell your audience they must take action with you. In fact, do your best to avoid making this statement at all. Speak objectively to your audience and they will gain trust and respect for you.

MASTERING THE ART OF "EDUCAINMENT"

As the name suggests, "educainment" is education that is made more enjoyable because it is entertaining. A variety of elements transform education into "educainment," including the following:

1. Stories. Tell stories about real people and real situations to maintain your audience's interest and attention while you illus-trate your points. Keep in mind that "educainment" stories are not merely case studies or examples, they have an emotional or humorous quality to them.

Make your stories come alive by adding some drama. Don't just tell the story. Sell the story. Practice alone until you can tell your stories artfully.

You should also keep a journal of new stories as you hear them. Even if you don't know whether you are going to use a particular piece or not, you can use it at a later date if you write it down. You should also give your stories names like the "Uncle Nat Story" or "My Sister Nancy Story." Make notes in your seminar leaders guide to remind yourself when to tell each story during the seminar.

2. Participation. As was described in Chapter 5, it is important to give your audience an opportunity to participate in the seminar with activities such as quizzes, discussion, calculations, and fill-in-the-blank workbook formats. For example, you can give people brain-teasers, have a contest and give a prize, play a game, do a role play, use props, do a magic trick, or any number of other creative activities.

Generally, your audience will be supportive if they find the activities fun, entertaining and relevant to the program. Even if it isn't totally successful, it will liven up the room sufficiently and that alone makes it worthwhile.

3. Use media. You can show a short (two- or three-minute) film clip to make a relevant point. Choose a clip that is particularly entertaining. You can also use a short recorded music clip to convey a feeling or make a point.

4. Quotes and poems. The best way to be profound without seeming pompous is by using another person's words. Even a Mark Twain quote such as, "A banker is a fellow who lends you his umbrella when the sun is shining and wants it back the minute it starts to rain," can work well to make a point in an entertaining way.

5. Humor. You don't have to be a comedian to give a good seminar, but it is important to make a conscious effort to inject some lightness into your presentation. Financial seminars can be intense. Give people a chance to loosen up a bit.

There is another very important reason to include humor into your presentation. Humor allows people to let their defenses down to some degree. The old-school salesperson always had a batch of new jokes to tell before any selling took place. Humor puts people into a more receptive frame of mind.

You need not be able to tell a joke to be add humor to your presentation. You can try one or more of the following techniques:

a. Show slides or overhead transparencies of funny cartoons.
b. Learn a few one-liners that you can inject throughout the seminar.
c. Use funny quotes or analogies.
d. Use body language or exploit the tone of your voice.
e. Draw on humorous, real-life experiences.

Keep an eye out for humor that you can use in your seminar, and when you hear something that might work well, write it down in a journal. Then try it out. Practice your timing and delivery until it really works.

Make it a point to add humor to your seminar presentation. Just be sure to keep your humor on the topic and relevant to the point you are making.

Caution: Make sure your humor is acceptable. Many forms of humor put down someone or a particular group. Clean, nonoffensive humor is hard to come by. Before you use any humor, scrutinize it very carefully. There are two types of humor that you can use: observational and self-deprecating. Observational humor is largely the kind of humor Bill Cosby uses; self-deprecating humor makes you the object of the joke. If the humor you find doesn't fit into one of these topics, *don't use it*.

RESOURCES

The Executive Speechwriter Newsletter is a great source for humor that is witty and funny and totally appropriate for financial seminars.

The Executive Speechwriter Newsletter
Emerson Falls
St. Johnsbury, VT 05819
(802) 748-4472

HOW TO HANDLE Q AND A LIKE A PRO

Questions are a golden opportunity for achieving your goals. The audience appreciates the chance to participate in the program, and you will build rapport and position yourself as an expert if you handle Q and A sessions properly.

Ideally you have created an atmosphere that encourages participants to ask questions throughout the presentation. When the answers to the questions are short and are relevant to the information being discussed, it is best to answer the questions immediately. If the answers require more time, it's best to defer your answer to the latter portion of the program. You also have the option of saying, "I'd like to answer that question after we're finished with the seminar. Is that OK with you?

The following are some general rules for conducting Q and A sessions:

1. Make an effort to keep answers as short as possible.
2. Take questions from different areas of the audience.
3. Get in the habit of paraphrasing the question and repeating it back to the audience. This will confirm to the person asking the question that you understand it and it will also give you a few extra moments to provide the best response.
4. Do not ask the questioner for approval of your answer. Chances are this person will not be completely satisfied and you risk getting into an extensive dialogue.
5. As you complete your answer to a question, break your eye contact and move on to someone else.
6. Always be willing to say, "I don't know," rather than bluff an answer.

HOW TO GET REALLY GOOD

Practically anyone can read a script and perform adequately as a seminar leader. With a moderate amount of dedication to the process, many people can do a good job. All financial industry professionals must make a commitment to getting good. Your bottom line depends on it.

Getting really good is the level at which delivering your seminar becomes an art and a science, and doing so substantially increases your success ratio. The following are the three most effective ways to improve your own performance and get *really* good.

1. Attend other seminars and hear other speakers. You will learn by observing and critiquing. Observe a variety of speakers and presenters. Watch talk show hosts, politicians, college professors, business leaders, and so forth. You will identify behaviors that you will want to avoid. You will also identify the skills and characteristics that you want to emulate.

2. Video and audiotape your own presentation. You'll make a quantum leap the first few times you watch and listen to yourself on tape, as you observe behavior that you were unaware of and quickly make the necessary changes.

3. Ask for critiques. You will be amazed at the great information you will receive that you never could have found out unless you asked for comments. Ask people you trust and who are supportive of your work as a seminar leader. Ask them, "What did you like? What could I have done differently to improve my presentation? What did you like most about my presentation? What did you like least?"

4. Get professional help. There are a variety of ways you can get professional help to improve your skills as a seminar leader. You can hire a coach who will give you personal attention, much like a tennis coach or a golf coach. Some of the best speakers in the world use coaches on a regular basis to improve and polish their performance.

There are also a variety of classes you can take that can improve your ability to deliver seminars. An acting class will help you improve you ability to tell stories; a stand-up comedy class will help you improve your ability to tell a joke; or a voice development course will enable you to improve the vocal component of your presentation. Of course, the Dale Carnegie Course is still considered one of the best ways to work on the basics in a workshop setting. This is a 12-week course that meets once a week. Each participant has the opportunity to speak every week.

Dale Carnegie and Associates, Inc.
1475 Franklin Ave.
Garden City, NY 11530
(516) 248-5100

5. Join professional associations. The following three associations can provide ongoing support and education for your development. They each offer workshops, conferences, newsletters, books, and tapes to aid you in developing your public presentation skills.

American Seminar Leaders Association
206 Sacramento St., Suite 201
Nevada City, CA 95959
(800) 735-0511
Fax (916) 265-2685

National Speakers Association
1500 S. Priest Drive
Tempe, AZ 85281
(602) 968-2552
Fax (602) 968-0911

Toastmasters International
P.O. Box 9052
Mission Viejo, CA 92690
(714) 858-8255

Getting Your Butterflies to Fly in Formation

NINE STEPS TO CONQUERING NERVOUSNESS

Even the most seasoned seminar leader can get butterflies before beginning a presentation. But in order to be effective, you must learn a few techniques that will chase those butterflies away.

According to the *Book of Lists*, fear of public speaking is the number one worst human fear. Believe it or not, heights, insects, money problems, sickness, and death are all less frightening to the average person. Nervousness is a universal response to public speaking and its can paralyze you or severely diminish the effectiveness of your delivery if you fail to do anything about it.

The first important underlying concept you must grasp is the physical nature of stress. Dr. Hans Selye, winner of the Nobel Prize for his research and author of *Stress Without Distress*, has analyzed the effect of stress on the human body. Selye describes the stress response, or "fight or flight" syndrome, as "the response of the body to any demand made upon it." The perception of danger causes the secretion of a variety of hormones into the bloodstream, of which the most powerful is adrenaline. Adrenaline produces a dramatic effect on the functions of the human body: muscles tighten, sweating occurs, the mouth goes dry, and the heartbeat and breathing rates increase. Once upon a time, this physical response served as a survival mechanism for the human species.

Do any of these physical reactions sound familiar? If you've ever spoken in public, you have probably experienced one or more of these reactions. When athletes are under pressure, the fight or flight response that affects them most is the tightening of muscles, which can cause a less-than-ideal performance. When a seminar leader stands before an audience "choking," it is quite literal. The muscles in the throat tighten and speaking becomes difficult and, in some cases, almost impossible.

The following are nine sure-fire ways to maintain control and overcome nervousness:

1. Prepare thoroughly for your presentation. Feeling confident is largely a result of being familiar with your material. There's an old joke about a tourist in New York who asks a young hipster, "How do I get to Carnegie Hall?" His response was, "Practice, man, practice!" Every great performer needs to review over and over the material that will be presented.

Even after you have presented your seminar many times, chances are you will want to keep your notes handy. You will constantly update and revise your seminar according to the audience's feedback, and you will need to make a variety of adjustments to accommodate these changes. Always make sure you are properly prepared for these changes *before* you begin your presentation.

2. Focus on your mission. Nervousness can be an all-consuming experience. Yet, your mission when presenting a financial seminar is really about positively affecting the lives of those in your audience. Remember, your goal is to *establish business relationships.* Focus your attention on providing your audience with an opportunity to take advantage of financial products and services. Concentrate on these goals instead of on yourself, and your nervousness will be greatly reduced.

3. Make friends with your audience. One of the most important techniques for reducing nervousness is to develop rapport with the members of your audience before the event begins. Circulate among the participants of your seminar before it begins. Introduce yourself and get to know them by name. When it comes time to step up to the front of the room, you will have a group of

friendly faces in front of you who you can glance at, call on, or refer to during the seminar to help you relax.

Besides increasing your closing ratios, contact with your audience before the event will allow you the opportunity to get to know your audience as individuals instead of as the "audience." The "audience" is a faceless entity. On the other hand, individuals have names like Kathy, Frank, and Tony, and together these individuals make up your audience.

4. Remember, the audience wants you to do well. You and your audience will be sharing time together at the seminar. Your audience is internally cheering for you.

Yes, your audience will be evaluating you. That's good for you, because evaluations are important. It will provide you with the feedback that will help you make improvements on the quality of your seminar. However, the majority of your audience are also saying to themselves, "I've invested some time to come to this seminar. I hope I have a good experience and the seminar leader does a good job." If you doubt this is true, ask for a volunteer to help you distribute your workbooks or move a couple of chairs. I guarantee many people will invariably want to contribute to your success.

5. Visualize and affirm your success. Positive thoughts produce positive results. Program yourself for success.

Visualize your seminar as you would like it to be. Remember to enlist the aid of all your senses when you visualize. *See* how you and the audience will look, *hear* your voice and how the participants respond and *feel* the relaxed energy you will be feeling during the seminar.

Focus on one or two simple phrases that will affirm a positive experience for you and your audience. Internal affirmations like "I'm glad I'm here," or "I'm glad you're here," or "You're glad I'm here," or "I'm going to have fun and so will my audience," work extremely well. Repeat such phrases to yourself a few times before you get up to speak.

6. Channel your physical energy. Don't forget nervousness is a physical manifestation and you must deal with it physically.

Yes, nervousness can scramble your thoughts, but it is also a real physical problem. The fight or flight syndrome is the physical response your body has to your nervousness. When you address the physical manifestations of nervousness, you will reduce its potential for negatively affecting your seminar.

There are a wide variety of techniques you can use to channel your physical energy. Arrive at your seminar room at least one hour before the program and move around the room. Physically circulate as people arrive. If you have time and the weather permits, take a few minutes to take a brisk walk outside. During the seminar itself, move around the room and use gestures to release energy.

7. Deep breathing. Just before you get up to deliver your presentation, make sure you spend at least three to five minutes breathing from your diaphragm. Shallow chest breathing increases the stress response, while "belly" breathing will relax you and help you gain composure.

8. Make eye contact with individuals. It is important to make eye contact and hold it for at least five seconds at a time during your seminar. Eye contact will focus your attention and connect your brain and body to your audience. The eye-brain connection reduces outside distractions and allows you to speak to one person. The five-second pause limits the stimuli to the brain, thereby reducing the "fight or flight" response. This technique also reduces stress by transforming a group presentation into a series of one-on-one conversations. Radio broadcasters use this trick when they visualize speaking to one person instead of one million.

9. Identify your own formula. Surveys conducted by The Business Institute have shown that people who are successful at controlling nervousness have created a unique personal plan for solving this problem. Stories abound concerning athletes who have lucky socks, who must lace their sneakers in some precise manner, or who eat "magic" foods before the competition. Exotic rituals and procedures to guarantee peak performance are not at all that unusual, and although these procedures seem off-the-wall, they do work.

You must experiment to find what works for you. Identify the factors that help you to relax before a presentation. Start with the proven winners that are outlined in this chapter, but don't be afraid to try new ideas or create your own combination of techniques. Remember, nervousness is a common and natural reaction that you can control.

HOW TO DEAL WITH DIFFICULT SEMINAR PARTICIPANTS

Every successful salesperson has the skills to gain and maintain control of the sales process. Seminar selling requires the same skills. Difficult participants can take control of your seminar and rob you of the opportunity to achieve your objectives. To avoid losing control it is important to familiarize yourself with a few simple, yet powerful, techniques and scripts that will keep difficult participants at bay.

These people fall into a few general categories. The following are the most common types of troublemakers and the specific techniques you can use to minimize their negative effects.

The loudmouth. There are two varieties of loudmouths: a supporter who is interested in your program and is overzealous, or someone who really doesn't care about you and is mostly interested in hearing his or her own voice. In both cases, the end result is the same: your program will be dominated, disturbed, and detoured by this individual. Here are the primary scenarios you must contend with and the best solution for each.

Scenario: Loudmouth raises hand and rambles on.

Solution: After a few moments ask, "What is your question?" or "What is your main point?" or "I appreciate your comments and insights, but I'd also like to hear from some of the others here today."

Scenario: Loudmouth asks vague questions or ones that are off the topic.

Solution: Say, "That's a good question, but it in order to cover all the material in our allotted time, I'd like to stick to our topic of _____." Or say, "Good question, but how does it relate to our topic?" Or say, "You are raising some interesting issues. They're a little off the material we are covering, but perhaps we can talk more at the break."

Scenario: Loudmouth raises hand continually every few minutes.

Solution: Avoid looking in the direction of the loudmouth.

The know-it-all.   At every financial seminar, a majority of your participants will have some degree of familiarity with the topic. Participants might get their information from personal contact or as a result of attending similar seminars. The know-it-all feels compelled to share his or her viewpoint every step of the way.

Scenario: The know-it-all repeatedly questions the validity or correctness of your information.

Solution: Prepare yourself with facts, figures, quotes, and other expert testimony. After you have delivered your seminar a few times, you will be able to better equipped to handle this type of troublemaker. You'll become more familiar with the areas that are likely to arouse opposing viewpoints.

Another solution: If you know there will be someone with an extensive background on your topic, speak with them before you begin. Acknowledge their expertise, experience, or credentials and ask this person for their support. This way, you can transform a potential enemy into an ally. Using this technique, the know-it-all will most likely be supportive instead of disagreeable.

The cross-talker. The cross-talker is someone who is attending your seminar with an associate, is seated next to someone they know, or has made a new friend at your seminar. In some cases the cross-talker will be commenting negatively to a neighbor, but in many cases they are making editorial comments.

The cross-talker is a distraction. This person will become your competition and, in most cases, will negate the quality of the seminar experience for those sitting nearby.

Scenario: A steady stream of whispering is emanating from the cross-talker.

Solution: Walk up close to the cross-talker and make eye contact.

Another solution: Stop talking and let the dead silence echo in the room.

Another solution: Deal with it head-on and say, "Excuse me, I'd like to ask you to refrain from cross-talk. It can disturb those around you and affect their experience. Out of respect for your fellow participants, please share with your colleagues at the break or when we are finished."

The silent one. The silent one can manifest in a few ways. The silent one can be observed sitting with his or her arms crossed with a blank stare, doodling incessantly, shaking his or her head, or fidgeting in a chair. This nonverbal behavior will communicate disinterest in one form or another.

The silent one can subtly sabotage your efforts to gain participation and maintain attention from the rest of your audience. The behavior of this person will negatively affect those around them.

Scenario: Participant is not involved in your presentation.

Solution: The best technique is to call on this person by name and ask an open-ended question, ask for their opinion, or ask for their direct input in some way.

Another solution: Speak with the silent one at the break. Find out exactly what is going on and develop a strategy that will gain his or her involvement. Try to find some way you can be of service to the participant. At this point the silent one might actually decide to leave on his or her own accord, realizing that being there is a waste of time.

The hostile one.   There can be lots of reasons for someone's hostility. The hostile person either is temporarily under the weather or it is this person's normal disposition. If you have behaved responsibly as a seminar leader, you have done nothing to create the hostile participant. Likewise, there is little you can do to make this person happy.

Your objective in handling the hostile participant is to diffuse the negativity and prevent the hostile one from taking control of your seminar. No matter what happens, do not lose your cool. If you do, you will lose the support of your audience.

Scenario: The hostile one is belligerent about something you've said.

Solution: Get agreement on some larger concept of your presentation. Say, "Although we disagree on some details, I'm sure you'll agree _____."

Another solution: If you see a pattern of this behavior right from the start, ask for a commitment from the audience. Before you've gone very far, say to the audience, "I'd like you to keep an open mind and hold your comments or questions till the end, when I will be happy to answer them."

If the hostile one tries to interrupt after you have said this, remind the hostile one of the verbal contract that was agreed to earlier. At this point, you'll probably have the audience on your side.

Undoubtedly, you will become quite familiar with each of these common seminar participant types. As a professional seminar leader, you must be prepared to deal with the troublemakers. After using these techniques and scripts a few times, they'll become much easier to apply as needed.

Remember, if you lose control of your audience, you lose control of the sale.

PART

II

RESOURCE
DIRECTORY

Financial Industry Publications

Here is a list of banking, finance, and insurance publications that will provide helpful information for planning your financial seminar.

Banking Publications

ABA Banking Journal
345 Hudson Street
New York, NY 10014-4590
(212) 620-7210

This journal is targeted toward middle and senior bank managers and offers information on how to manage a bank profitably.

American Banker
One State Street Plaza
New York, NY 10004-1549
(212) 943-5710

Targeted toward senior executives, this publication deals with current banking conditions and changes.

Bank Director
P.O. Box 1603
Brentwood, TN 37024-1603
(615) 790-6886

This publication, targeted toward bank directors, focuses on strategic issues in banking.

Bank Investment Marketing
40 West 57th Street, 11th Floor
New York, NY 10019
(212) 765-5311

This publication provides insights and analysis for bank securities and insurance professionals.

Bank Management
118 S. Clinton, #700
Chicago, IL 60601
(312) 648-0261

This publication is targeted toward administrative personnel and covers all areas of bank management.

Bank Marketing
309 W. Washington
Chicago, IL 60606-3273
(312) 782-1442

Targeted toward all people involved in bank marketing, this publication covers topics related to the development and use of marketing techniques.

Bank Technology News
Eleven Penn Plaza
New York, NY 10001
(212) 967-7000

This publication aims to educate all bank personnel of new products and features in the banking arena.

The Bankers Magazine
One Penn Plaza, 42nd Floor
New York, NY 10119-0018
(212) 971-5226

Targeted toward senior bankers and CEOs, this publication covers a wide variety of current banking topics.

Bankers Monthly
200 W. 57th Street, 15th Floor
New York, NY 10019-3283
(212) 399-1084

Targeted toward all banking and investment professionals, this publication covers trends in the financial markets and bank management and marketing.

Banks in Insurance Report
22 West 21st Street
New York, NY 10010
(212) 645-7880

This publication is targeted toward bank executives and reports on industry news and events.

The Community Bank President
P.O. Box 1384
Storm Lake, IA 50588-1384
(712) 732-7340

Targeted toward senior management, this publication focuses on banking products and news.

Financial Woman Today
7910 Woodmont Avenue, #1430
Bethesda, MD 20814
(301) 657-8288

Targeted toward women, this publication deals with both finance and personal issues.

The Independent Banker
P.O. Box 267
Sauk Centre, MN 56378-0267
(612) 352-6546

For members of the Independent Bankers Association of America, this publication offers information on new products and industry news.

*International Investment
and Banking Report*
215 Park Avenue South, 15th Floor
New York, NY 10003-1603
(212) 460-0600

This publication covers industry news.

The Journal of Commercial Lending
One Liberty Place, #2300
Philadelphia, PA 19103
(215) 851-9144

Targeted toward credit professionals, this publication provides information related exclusively to lending.

Mortgage Banking
1125 15th Street, NW, 6th Floor
Washington, DC 20005-2766
(202) 861-6562

Targeted toward executives in investment firms, this publication deals with current economic and political news affecting the industry.

Savings Institutions
1709 New York Avenue, NW
Washington, DC 20006
(202) 637-8900

Targeted toward management level personnel in operations, this publication focuses on techniques in bank management.

United States Banker
60 East 42nd Street, #3810
New York, NY 10165
(212) 599-3310

This publication covers financial news and trends and is targeted toward senior management in the banking and financial industry.

Financial Publications

Across the Board
845 Third Avenue
New York, NY 10022-6601
(212) 759-0900

The content of this publication includes industry news and trends.

Bank Investment Representative
632 North Main, Suite 1C
P.O. Box 4364
Logan, UT 84323-4364
(801) 752-1173

This publication focuses on investment marketing and investment program management.

Barron's National Business and Financial Weekly
Dow Jones & Company
200 Liberty Street
New York, NY 10281
(212) 416-2000

This publication focuses on general business and financial news.

Bloomberg Magazine
P.O. Box 888
Princeton, NJ 08542-0888
(609) 252-8352

This publication covers financial industry news and new products.

The Bond Buyer
One State Street Plaza
New York, NY 10004-1505
(212) 943-8410

Targeted toward financial industry professionals, this publication covers tax-exempt bonds and new issues.

Bull & Bear Financial Newspaper
P.O. Box 917179
Longwood, FL 32791
(407) 682-6170

This publication features information on stocks, gold commodities, mutual funds, currencies, and economic trends.

Business Credit
8815 Centre Park Drive, #200
Columbia, MD 21045-2144
(410) 740-5560

The topics covered in this publication include business credit trends and company finance.

CFO Magazine
253 Summer Street
Boston, MA 02210-1118
(617) 345-9700

Targeted toward senior financial executives, the content of this publication focuses on insurance, benefits, taxation, and cash management.

CFP Today
7600 E. Eastman Avenue, #301
Denver, CO 80231
(303) 751-7600

This publication focuses on financial industry news, events, and new products.

Computerized Investing
625 N. Michigan Avenue, #1900
Chicago, IL 60611-3109
(312) 280-0170

This publication is targeted toward the individual investors using computers for analysis.

Corporate Finance
1328 Broadway
New York, NY 10001
(212) 594-5030

Targeted toward senior management at larger corporations, this publication provides financial ideas, case studies, and personnel overviews.

Credit Union Executive
P.O. Box 431
Madison, WI 53701-0431
(608) 231-4094

This quarterly publication for the Credit Union National Association covers industry news.

Credit Union Magazine
P.O. Box 431
Madison, WI 53701-0431
(608) 231-4000

Targeted toward credit union executives and staff, this publication covers all aspects of the credit union industry.

Credit Union Management
P.O. Box 14167
Madison, WI 53714-0167
(608) 271-2664

Published by the Credit Union Executives Society, this publication features new products and industry news.

Credit Union News
150 Nassau Street, #2030
New York, NY 10038-1516
(212) 267-7707

Targeted toward credit union executives, topics in this publication include financial and technical concerns.

Donoghue's Moneyletter
P.O. Box 91004
Ashland, MA 01721-9104
(508) 881-2800

This publication provides industry news and new products.

Equities
37 East 28th Street, #706
New York, NY 10016-7969

The content of this publication includes industry news and new product information.

Estate Planning
One Penn Plaza, 40th Floor
New York, NY 10119-0118
(212) 971-5000

This publication is targeted toward professionals in estate planning and family asset management.

FACS of the Week: Mutual Fund News and Information
260 Franklin Street
Boston, MA 02110-3112
(617) 439-6195

This publication focuses on new products, industry news, personnel and events.

Federal Credit Union
3138 N. 10th Street
Arlington, VA 22201-2149
(703) 522-4770

This bimonthly publication covers new products and events.

Financial Analysts Journal
200 Park Avenue, 18th Floor
New York, NY 10166
(212) 953-5700

Targeted toward professional investors, this publication reports on policies and developments in the industry.

Financial Executive
10 Madison Avenue
Morristown, NJ 07962-1938
(201) 898-4600

This publication covers current financial issues and strategies.

Financial Planning
40 West 57th Street, 8th Floor
New York, NY 10019-4001
(212) 765-5311

This publication covers events and trends in the financial industry, including new products and concepts.

Financial Services Week
2 World Trade Center, 18th Floor
New York, NY 10048

This publication is targeted toward retail financial product and services executives.

Financial World
1328 Broadway, 3rd Floor
New York, NY 10001
(212) 594-5030

This publication focuses on business, financial, and economic topics.

Global Finance
55 John Street
New York, NY 10038-3712
(212) 766-5868

Targeted toward corporate financial executives, bankers, and money managers, this publication provides information on cross-border transactions.

Going Public: The IPO Reporter
2 World Trade Center, 18th Floor
New York, NY 10048-0203
(212) 227-1200

Published by the Investment Dealers Digest, this publication provides finance news.

Individual Investor
38 East 29th Street, 4th Floor
New York, NY 10016-7911
(212) 689-2777

This publication is targeted toward investors, brokers, dealers, and analysts interested in stocks.

Institutional Investor; Institutional Investor, International Edition
488 Madison Avenue
New York, NY 10022-5751
(212) 303-3300

These publications are targeted toward investors and consumers interested in the current status of the investment world.

Investment Advisor
179 Avenue at the Common, 2nd Floor
Shrewsbury, NJ 07702
(908) 389-8700

This newsmagazine is targeted toward independent financial advisors and features mutual funds, annuities, and investment products.

Investment Executive
129 Garfield Avenue
Toronto, Ontario M4T 1G2
Canada
(416) 932-2024

This publication focuses on financial industry news.

The Investment Reporter
325 N. Newport
Newport Beach, CA 92663
(714) 548-8035

This publication focuses on financial industry news.

Journal of Financial Planning
7600 E. Eastman Avenue, #301
Denver, CO 80231-4397
(303) 751-7600

This publication reports on trends across the financial planning industry.

The Journal of Taxation
One Penn Plaza, 41st Floor
New York, NY 10119-0132
(212) 971-5185

This journal provides news within the tax industry.

Money Management Letter
488 Madison Avenue, 12th Floor
New York, NY 10022-5702
(212) 303-3362

This biweekly publication features industry news.

Mutual Fund Forecaster
3471 N. Federal Highway
Fort Lauderdale, FL 33306-1088
(305) 563-9000

This publication is published by The Institute for Econometric Research.

Registered Representative
18818 Teller Avenue, #280
Irvine, CA 92715-1600
(714) 851-2220

Targeted toward financial service representatives, this publication features industry trends and developments.

Research
2201 Third Street
San Francisco, CA 94107-3125
(415) 621-0220

This investment product magazine is targeted toward stock brokers and branch managers.

Securities Product News
Two World Trade Center, 18th Floor
New York, NY 10048
(212) 227-1200

This quarterly publication features industry news, new products, and personnel.

Securities Week
1221 Avenue of the Americas
New York, NY 10020-1001
(212) 512-6148

This publication focuses on new products and industry news.

Strategic Investment
824 E. Baltimore Street
Baltimore, MD 21202-4702
(410) 234-0515

This publication features investment industry news.

The Tax Advisor
1211 Avenue of the Americas
New York, NY 10036-8775
(212) 575-6313

This publication is targeted toward public accountants, attorneys, financial executives, and tax practitioners.

*Technical Analysis of Stocks
and Commodities*
3517 SW Alaska Street
Seattle, WA 98126-2700
(206) 938-0570

This publication features industry news and new products.

Trusts and Estates
6255 Barfield Road, #100
Atlanta, GA 30328-4318
(404) 256-9800

This publication features financial trade literature and events.

Insurance Publications

American Agent and Broker
330 N. Fourth
St. Louis, MO 63102-2729
(314) 421-5445

Targeted toward independent property-casualty insurance agents and brokers, this publication provides sales, management, and technical information.

*Best's Review, Life/Health
Insurance Edition*
Ambest Road
Oldwick, NJ 08858
(908) 439-2200

This publication is for members of
the casualty insurance industry and
focuses on trends.

Broker World
10709 Barkley, #3
Overland Park, KS 66211
(913) 383-9191

This publication is targeted toward
insurance sales professionals involved
with health and life coverage.

Business Insurance
740 Rush Street
Chicago, IL 60611-2525
(312) 649-5398

Targeted toward risk/benefit insurance executives, this publication features new policies, trends, and news.

GAMA News Journal
1922 F Street, NW
Washington, DC 20006-4389
(202) 223-5533

This publication features trade articles
and industry news.

The Health Insurance Underwriter
1000 Connecticut Avenue, #1111
Washington, DC 20036-5302
(202) 331-6088

This is the official publication of
the National Association of Health
Underwriters and is targeted toward
disability income and health insurance
agents and brokers.

Independent Agent
127 S. Peyton Street
Alexandria, VA 22314-2803
(703) 706-5411

This publication is targeted toward
full-time professional insurance
agents and brokers.

Insurance Review
2 World Trade Center, 27th Floor
New York, NY 10048
(212) 837-7090

This publication reports news, issues,
and developments within the casual
insurance industry.

*Journal of the American Society
of CLU and CHFC*
270 Bryn Mawr Avenue
Bryn Mawr, PA 19010
(215) 526-2500

This publication features trade literature and industry news.

Life and Health Insurance Sales
P.O. Box 564
Indianapolis, IN 46206-0564
(317) 634-1541

This publication is targeted toward
life and health insurance agents and
covers current events, sales and client
development techniques, underwriting, and public relations tips.

Life Association News
1922 F Street, NW
Washington, DC 20006-4387
(202) 331-6070

This publication is targeted toward
individual life and health insurance
agents.

Life Insurance Selling
330 N. Fourth
St. Louis, MO 63102-2729
(314) 421-5445

Targeted toward life insurance sales-people, this publication provides information on current trends, sales techniques, and new policy developments.

Limra's Marketfacts
P.O. Box 208
Hartford, CT 06141-0208
(203) 677-0033

This publication features new products and industry news.

National Underwriter, Life and Health Insurance Edition
43–47 Newark Street
Hoboken, NJ 07030-5604
(201) 963-2300

Targeted toward professionals in the life and health insurance industry, this publication provides information on stocks and marketing.

National Underwriter, Property and Casualty Insurance Edition
43–47 Newark Street
Hoboken, NJ 07030-5604
(201) 963-2300

Targeted toward professionals in the property and casualty insurance industry, this publication covers trends, risk management and judicial affairs.

Professional Agent
400 N. Washington Street
Alexandria, VA 22314-2353
(703) 836-9340

This publication is published by the National Association of Professional Insurance Agents.

Professional Insurance Agents
25 Chamberlain Street
Glenmont, NY 12077-0997
(518) 434-3111

This publication features new products, events, and industry news.

Resource
5770 Powers Ferry Road
Atlanta, GA 30327-4350
(404) 951-1770

Targeted toward home and field office personnel in life insurance management, this publication covers administrative and managerial topics.

Today's Insurance Woman
1847 East 15th Street
Tulsa, OK 74104-4610
(918) 744-5195

This publication is targeted toward professional insurance women and focuses on management and social issues facing women in the industry.

Banking, Finance, and Insurance Associations

Banking Associations

American Bankers Association
1120 Connecticut Avenue, NW
Washington, DC 20036
(202) 663-5000

This organization is for all employees within the banking industry.

Consumers Bankers Association
1000 Wilson Boulevard, 30th Floor
Arlington, VA 22209-3908
(703) 276-1750

This is an association for federally insured deposit-taking institutions.

Electronic Funds Transfer Association
950 Herndon Parkway, Suite 390
Herndon, VA 22073
(703) 435-9800

This organization provides a forum for those involved with electronic funds systems products and services.

Farm Credit Council
50 F Street, NW, Suite 900
Washington, DC 20001
(202) 626-8710

This organization promotes the interests of agricultural lending institutions.

Financial Women International
500 N. Michigan Avenue, Suite 1400
Chicago, IL 60611
(312) 661-1700

This association is for women officers and managers in the banking industry.

Forex U.S.A.
Tradition Berisford L.P.
61 Broadway
New York, NY 10006
(212) 797-5580

This association is for those involved in the foreign exchange industry.

Independent Bankers Association of America
1 Thomas Circle, NW, Suite 950
Washington, DC 20005
(202) 659-8111

This is an association for small and medium sized community banks.

Institute of Financial Education
111 East Wacker Drive, 9th Floor
Chicago, IL 60601-4680
(312) 946-8800

This organization conducts courses for bank personnel nationwide.

Institute of International Bankers
299 Park Avenue, 38th Floor
New York, NY 10171
(212) 421-1611

This organization provides support for non-U.S. banks with officers in the United States.

Institute of International Finance
2000 Pennsylvania Avenue, NW, Suite 8500
Washington, DC 20006
(202) 857-3600

This is an organization for international lending organizations.

International Union of Housing Finance Institutions
111 East Wacker Drive, Suite 900
Chicago, IL 60601
(312) 946-8201

This is an association for private and publicly owned thrift and home financing institutions in 60 nations.

Mortgage Bankers Association of America
1125 15th Street, NW
Washington, DC 20005
(202) 861-6500

This organization is for members of the mortgage finance field.

National Association for Bank Cost and Management Accounting
P.O. Box 458
Northbrook, IL 60065-0458
(708) 272-4233

This organization is for employees of banks, trust companies, and credit unions interested in cost analysis and management accounting.

National Association of Mortgage Brokers
706 East Bell Road, Suite 101
Phoenix, AZ 85022
(602) 992-6181

This is a networking group strictly for mortgage brokers.

National Association of Urban Bankers
122 C Street, NW, Suite 500-B
Washington, DC 20001
(202) 783-4743

This organization is for minority professionals in the financial services industry.

National Automated Clearing House Association
607 Herndon Parkway, Suite 200
Herndon, VA 22070
(703) 742-9190

This organization conducts national seminars and sponsors an annual Payments Institute.

National Bankers Association
122 C Street, NW, Suite 580
Washington, DC 20001
(202) 783-3200

This organization is for minority banks or minority employees of majority banks.

National Council of Savings Institutions
1101 15th Street, NW, Suite 400
Washington, DC 20005
(202) 857-3100

This association is for all savings and loan institutions, and sponsors the National School of Finance and Management.

Finance Associations

Credit Card Users of America
P.O. Box 7100
Beverly Hills, CA 90212
(818) 343-4434

This is an association for credit card holders and companies.

Credit Professionals International
50 Crestwood Exec Center, Suite 204
St. Louis, MO 63126
(314) 842-6280

This is an organization for employees in credit or collection departments of firms.

Credit Research Foundation
8815 Center Park Drive
Columbia, MD 21045
(301) 740-5499

This organization is for credit and financial executives.

Direct Marketing Credit Association
Reader's Digest
Pleasantville, NY 10570
(914) 241-5175

This is an organization for credit professionals in the mail order industry.

Eastern Finance Association
Georgia Southern University
Department of Finance
P.O. Box 8151
Statesboro, GA 30460
(912) 681-5437

This organization provides meeting space for anyone interested in financial topics. Sponsors awards.

Financial Executives Institute
10 Madison Avenue
P.O. Box 1938
Morristown, NJ 07962-1938
(201) 898-4600

This organization is for professional controllers, treasurers, and financial VPs.

Financial Executives Research Foundation
P.O. Box 1938
10 Madison Avenue
Morristown, NJ 07962-1938
(201) 898-4608

This organization conducts research in business management, emphasizing finance.

Financial Managers Society
8 S. Michigan Avenue, Suite 500
Chicago, IL 60603
(312) 578-1300

This organization is a technical information exchange for financial managers of financial institutions.

Financial Women's Association of New York
215 Park Avenue South, Suite 2010
New York, NY 10003
(212) 533-2141

This is an association for professional women in the finance field in the NYC metropolitan area.

Institute of Certified Financial Planners
7600 E. Eastman Avenue, Suite 301
Washington, DC 80231
(303) 751-7600

This organization is for those who have been designated CFPs.

International Association for Financial Planning
2 Concourse Parkway, Suite 800
Atlanta, GA 30328
(404) 395-1605

This organization is for individuals in 10 countries involved in the financial planning industry.

**International Association
of Registered Financial Planners**
305 East Franklin Avenue
El Paso, TX 79901
(915) 544-7947

This association is open to those
financial planners who have met
education, experience, and integrity
requirements.

International Credit Association
243 N. Lindbergh Boulevard
St. Louis, MO 63141
(314) 991-3030

This organization is for credit executives in the finance industry.

**International Newspaper
Financial Executives**
Dulles International Airport
P.O. Box 16573
Washington, DC 20041
(703) 648-1160

This organization is for controllers,
accountants, business managers, audi-
tors, treasurers, and related newspaper executives.

**International Board of Standards
and Practices for Certified
Financial Planners**
1660 Lincoln Street, Suite 3050
Denver, CO 80264
(303) 830-7543

This organization registers, tests, and
certifies financial planners with work
experience.

**National Association of Charitable
Estate Counselors**
P.O. Box 5359
Lake Worth, FL 33466
(407) 434-0100

This organization is for charitable
estate counselors, financial planners,
attorneys, and trust officers.

**National Association
of Corporate Treasurers**
1101 Connecticut Avenue, NW,
Suite 700
Washington, DC 20036
(202) 857-1115

This organization serves as a forum
for financial executives who perform
corporate treasurer duties.

**National Association
of Credit Management**
8815 Centre Park Drive
Columbia, MD 21045
(301) 740-5560

This association is for credit and
financial executives representing
manufacturers, wholesalers, insurance
companies, utilities, and the like.

**National Association of Estate
Planning Councils**
98 Dennis Drive
Lexington, KY 40503

This is an association for life underwriters, trust officers, attorneys, and
CPAs in the field of estate planning.

**National Association of Personal
Finance Advisors**
1130 Lake Cook Road, Suite 105
Buffalo Grove, IL 60089
(708) 537-7722

This is an organization for full-time,
fee-only financial planners.

**Registered Financial
Planners Institute**
2001 Cooper Foster Park Road
Amherst, OH 44001
(216) 282-7176

This association is for registered
financial planners.

**Society of Certified
Credit Executives**
P.O. Box 419057
St. Louis, MO 63141-1757
(314) 991-3030

This is a division of the International Credit Association (see separate listing).

**Society of Independent
Financial Advisors**
5954 S. Monaco Way
Englewood, CO 80111
(303) 850-9166

This is an organization for companies of independent personal financial advisors.

Treasury Management Association
7315 Wisconsin Avenue, Suite 1250W
Bethesda, MD 20814
(301) 907-2862

This organization sponsors Innovation in Treasury Management competition and conducts educational programs.

Women in Housing and Finance
655 15th Street, NW, Suite 300
Washington, DC 20005
(202) 639-4999

This organization is for professionals in the fields of housing and finance.

Insurance Associations

**American Institute
of Marine Underwriters**
14 Wall Street
New York, NY 10005
(212) 233-0550

This is an organization for marine insurance companies authorized to conduct business in one or more states.

**American Institute for Property
Casualty Underwriters**
720 Providence Road
Malvern, PA 19355-0770
(215) 644-2100

This organization determines qualifications for professional certification of insurance personnel.

American Insurance Association
1130 Connecticut Avenue, NW,
Suite 1000
Washington, DC 20036
(202) 828-7100

This association represents companies providing property and casualty insurance and suretyship.

**American Insurance
Services Group**
85 John Street
New York, NY 10038
(212) 669-0400

The members of this organization are companies involved in property casualty insurance.

**American Marine
Insurance Forum**
GRE/Talbot Bird
61 Broadway
New York, NY 10006
(212) 208-4200

This organization is for ocean marine insurance underwriters insuring hulls, cargoes, and similar risks.

**American Society of CLU
and CHFC**
270 Bryn Mawr Avenue
Bryn Mawr, PA 19010
(610) 526-2500

This organization is for agents and financial services professionals who hold CLU or CHFC designations.

**Associated Risk Managers
International**
200 Colorado Building
702 Colorado Street
Austin, TX 78701

This organization is for independent
insurance agencies that provide property and casualty insurance.

**Association for Advanced
Life Underwriting**
1922 F Street, NW
Washington, DC 20006
(202) 331-6081

This organization is for advanced life
underwriters who specialize in complex fields.

**Captive Insurance Companies
Association**
205 East 42nd Street
New York, NY 10017
(212) 687-4501

This organization's purpose is to
preserve information useful to firms
utilizing the captive insurance company.

**Conference of Casualty Insurance
Companies**
3601 Vincennes Road
P.O. Box 681098
Indianapolis, IN 46268
(317) 872-4061

This organization is for casualty
insurance companies.

**Consumer Credit Insurance
Association**
542 S. Dearborn, #400
Chicago, IL 60605
(312) 939-2242

This organization is for insurance
companies underwriting consumer
credit in areas of life, accident, health,
and property insurance.

**Council of Life Insurance
Consultants**
P.O. Box 803653
Chicago, IL 60680-3653
(800) 533-0777

This organization is for consumers,
accountants, attorneys, brokers, and
financial planners.

**Direct Marketing
Insurance Council**
11 West 42nd Street
New York, NY 10036
(212) 768-7277

This organization is for direct
response divisions of insurance companies.

**Disability Insurance
Training Council**
1000 Connecticut Avenue, NW,
Suite 1111
Washington, DC 20036
(202) 223-5533

This organization is an educational
arm of the National Association of
Health Underwriters.

**General Agents and Managers
Association**
1922 F Street, NW
Washington, DC 20006
(202) 331-6088

This organization is for life insurance
general agents and managers, assistant agency heads, and home office
officials.

**Health Insurance Association
of America**
1025 Connecticut Avenue, NW,
Suite 1200
Washington, DC 20036
(202) 223-7780

This organization is for health and
accident insurance firms.

**Independent Insurance Agents
of America**
127 South Peyton
Alexandria, VA 22314
(703) 683-4422

This organization is for sales agencies
handling casualty, fire, and surety
insurance.

**Inland Marine Underwriters
Association**
14 Wall Street
New York, NY 10005
(212) 233-7959

This organization is for insurance
companies transacting inland marine
insurance in the United States.

**Institute of Home Office
Underwriters**
Munich American Reassurance Co.
P.O. Box 3210
Atlanta, GA 30302
(404) 394-5665

This organization has a corporate
membership of home office life insurance underwriters.

**Insurance Accounting
and Systems Association**
P.O. Box 51340
Durham, NC 27717
(919) 489-0991

This organization is open to insurance companies writing all lines of
insurance.

**Insurance Industry Meetings
Association**
2330 S. Brentwood Boulevard
Suite 666
St. Louis, MO 63144-2096
(314) 961-2300

This association is for insurance companies and insurance company communications representatives.

Insurance Information Institute
110 William Street
New York, NY 10038
(212) 669-9200

This organization is for property and
liability insurance companies.

Insurance Institute of America
720 Providence Road
Malvern, PA 19355
(215) 644-2100

This organization sponsors educational programs for property and
liability insurance personnel.

**Insurance Marketing
Communications Association**
148 State Street, Suite 305
Boston, MA 02109
(617) 266-8400

This organization is for advertising,
public relations, and sales executives.

Insurance Research Council
1200 Harger Road, Suite 310
Oak Brook, IL 60521
(708) 572-1177

This is an organization for insurance
companies.

Insurance Services Office
7 World Trade Center
New York, NY 10048
(212) 898-6000

This organization is for property and
liability insurance companies.

Insurance Society of New York
101 Murray Street
New York, NY 10007
(212) 815-9217

International Claims Association
1701 First Avenue
Rock Island, IL 61201
(309) 786-6481

This organization is for claim executives representing companies writing life, health, or accident insurance.

International Insurance Council
1212 New York Avenue, Suite 250
Washington, DC 20005
(202) 682-2345

This organization is for companies and U.S. licensed trade associations that are risk-bearing companies.

**Life Insurance Marketing
and Research Association**
Box 208
Hartford, CT 06141
(203) 677-0033

This organization for life insurance companies conducts market, consumer, economic, and financial research.

Life Insurers Conference
The Pavillion
5770 Powers Ferry Rd., NW,
Suite 301
Atlanta, GA 30327
(404) 933-9954

This organization is for home service insurance agencies writing life, accident, and sickness insurance.

**Life Office Management
Association**
5770 Powers Ferry Road, NW
Atlanta, GA 30327
(404) 951-1770

This organization is for life and health insurance companies in the U.S. and Canada.

**National Association of Insurance
Women—International**
1847 East 15th
P.O. Box 4410
Tulsa, OK 74159
(918) 744-5195

This organization is for individuals in the insurance business.

American Council of Life Insurance
1455 Pennsylvania Avenue, NW,
Suite 1250
Washington, DC 20006
(202) 624-2000

This organization is for life and health insurance companies.

**National Association of Life
Underwriters**
1922 F Street, NW
Washington, DC 20006
(202) 331-6001

This is a federation of state and local associations representing life insurance agents, general agents, and managers.

**National Association of Mutual
Insurance Companies**
3606 Vincennes Road
P.O. Box 68700
Indianapolis, IN 46268-0700
(317) 875-5250

This association is for mutual property and casualty insurance companies.

**National Association of Professional
Insurance Agents**
400 N. Washington Street
Alexandria, VA 22314
(703) 836-9340

This is an organization for independent property and casualty insurance agents.

National Association of Public Insurance Adjusters
300 Water Street, Suite 400
Baltimore, MD 21202
(301) 539-4141

This is a professional society of public insurance adjusters.

National Committee on Property Insurance
10 Winthrop Square
Boston, MA 02110-1273
(617) 423-4620

This organization provides advice and assistance for insurance companies that write insurance coverages in distressed or residual insurance markets.

National Council on Compensation Insurance
One Penn Plaza
New York, NY 10119
(212) 560-1000

This organization is for insurance companies of all types writing workers' compensation insurance.

National Council of Self-Insurers
10 S. Riverside Plaza, Suite 1530
Chicago, IL 60606
(312) 454-5110

This organization is for state associations, individual companies, and others concerned with self-insurance under the workers' compensation laws.

Speakers Bureaus and Cruise Line Bureaus

Here is a list of speakers bureaus and cruise line bureaus, grouped by state, that can market your seminar for you.

Speakers Bureaus

Super Speakers of Alaska
P.O. Box 91120
Anchorage, AK 99509
Phone: (907) 338-1213
Contact: Ral West

Life at the Top Bureau
35095 Huntington Drive
Solotna, AK 99669-8308
Phone: (907) 262-6211
Contact: Laura Peterson

The Roundhouse
Box 13057
Huntsville, AL 35802
Phone: (205) 882-1737
Contact: Ruth A. Young

Access Speakers Bureau, Inc.
#8 Shackleford Plaza, Box 22668
Little Rock, AR 72221-2668
Phone: (501) 225-8667
Fax: (501) 225-8375
Contact: Barbara Vogel and
          Janice Peters

Standing Room Only
612 W. M Street
N. Little Rock, AR 72116-7229
Phone: (501) 771-5053
Contact: Virmarie Suria

Professional Speakers of America
8443 N. 34th Avenue
Phoenix, AZ 85051
Phone: (602) 973-2290
Fax: (602) 841-8953
Contact: Edward Zumach

Southwest Events
8233 Paseo Del Norte #E-600
Scottsdale, AZ 85258
Phone: (602) 991-5131
Contact: Bonnie Paulie

NewInformation Presentations
2248 South Forest
Tempe, AZ 85282
Phone: (602) 967-6070
Fax: (602) 967-1044
Contact: Bobette Gorden

Gold Stars Speakers Bureau
P.O. Box 37106
Tucson, AZ 85740
Phone: (602) 742-4384
Fax: (602) 797-3557
Contact: Andrea Gold

Praxis Speakers and Trainers
Box 44334
Tucson, AZ 85733-4334
Phone: (602) 887-8685
Fax: (602) 292-0779
Contact: Mary Billings

That's Entertainment Productions
1360 N. Hancock Street
Anaheim, CA 92807
Phone: (800) 321-1295
        (714) 693-9300
Fax: (714) 693-7963
Contact: John McEnte

California Speakers Bureau
11717 Palm Avenue
Bakersfield, CA 93312-3616
Phone: (805) 589-8301
Fax: (805) 589-8303
Contact: H. Stanley Jones, CPA, JD

Crest Organization
940 Emmett Avenue, #14
Belmont, CA 94002
Phone: (415) 595-2626
Contact: Ruth Self

Charman Speakers Bureau
4181 King Street, #69
Burbank, CA 91506
Phone: (818) 842-0170
Fax: (818) 842-0170
Contact: Linda Charman

Celebrity Gems
4061 E. Castro Valley Boulevard, #118
Castro Valley, CA 94552
Phone: (510) 581-5964
Contact: Stan Heimowitz

Robson Bureau
3 Barrier Reef Drive
Corona Del Mar, CA 92625
Phone: (714) 720-0343
Contact: Gail Robson

Orange County Speakers Bureau
11606 McDonald Street
Culver City, CA 92679-0230
Phone: (310) 313-6764
Contact: Terry and Joanne
        Van Hook

Age Wave, Inc.
1900 Powell Street, Suite 800
Emeryville, CA 94608
Phone: (510) 652-9099
Fax: (510) 652-8245

International Speakers Events and Media
4790 Irvine Boulevard
Suite 105-323
Irvine, CA 92720
Phone: (714) 669-1557
Contact: Carol Maree

Speaker Source
22 Woodleaf
Irvine, CA 92714
Phone: (714) 551-5710
Contact: Julie Kellar

Bernstein and Associates
7777 Fay Avenue, Suite K-278
LaJolla, CA 92037
Phone: (619) 459-8553
Fax: (619) 459-3580
Contact: Irv Bernstein

Financial Services Speakers Network
Box 8729
LaJolla, CA 92038-8729
Phone: (619) 622-2035
Fax: (619) 457-0973

Five Star Speakers—Western Region
219 Broadway, #355
Laguna Beach, CA 92651
Phone: (714) 376-9755
Fax: (714) 494-2211
Contact: Jeff Wood

Professional Artist's Contact Service
2033 Talmage Avenue
Los Angeles, CA 90027
Phone: (213) 665-7011
Contact: Don Snyder

Tannen, Herb—Assoc. Inc.
Talent Agency
1800 N. Vine, #120
Los Angeles, CA 90028
Phone: (213) 466-6191
Contact: Herb Tannen

The Leigh Bureau
11900 W. Olympic Boulevard, #670
Los Angeles, CA 90067-1151
Phone: (310) 442-9898
Fax: (310) 826-1065
Contact: Fern Webber

World Class Speakers Bureau
10747 Wilshire Boulevard, Suite 807
Los Angeles, CA 90024-4432
Phone: (310) 824-3333
Fax: (310) 470-2111
Contact: Joe Kessler

Convention Connection
18133 Coastline Drive, #3
Malibu, CA 90265
Phone: (310) 459-0159
Fax: (310) 454-2518
Contact: Suzanne Hill

Dynamic Speakers Bureau
Box 721
Malibu, CA 90265
Phone: (213) 457-2551
Fax: (213) 457-2652
Contact: Jay Klahn

Optimal Speakers
and Trainers Bureau
P.O. Box 12045
Marina Del Rey, CA 90295
Phone: (310) 578-0047
Fax: (310) 822-8750 (+99)
Contact: Rosalene Glickman

Golden Gate Speakers Bureau
International
P.O. Box 1336
Mill Valley, CA 94942-0508
Phone: (415) 383-5426/383-7306
Fax: (415) 381-8361
Contact: William Shear/Ann Roth

VAI—Speakers Division
Mojave Airport
1260 Flightline, Hangar 77
Mojave, CA 93501
Phone: (805) 824-4608
Fax: (805) 824-9575
Contact: Kelly Chandler

"INFOCOM"
P.O. Box 1147
Novato, CA 94948-1147
Phone: (415) 892-1530
Contact: Jim Gibson

"Let's Talk"
Terry L. Schutte and Associates
2624 Kingland Avenue
Oakland, CA 94619
Phone: (510) 533-3716
Fax: (510) 532-7252
Contact: Veronica Aiken

Speakers Bureau of the Desert
73572 Encelia
Palm Desert, CA 92260
Phone: (619) 568-2176
Contact: Gene Roberts
            Cheri Adams

Keynote Speakers, Inc.
425 Sherman, #200
Palo Alto, CA 94306-1823
Phone: (415) 325-8711
Fax: (415) 325-8737
Contact: Barbara Foster

Talk West
2332 Via Anacapa
Palos Verdes Estates, CA 90274
Phone: (310) 337-5668
Contact: Alice I. Boren

ProMark Service Bureau
115 W. California Boulevard, #285
Pasadena, CA 91105
Phone: (818) 578-0115
Fax: (818) 578-7334
Contact: Margarite Ave

West Coast Speakers Bureau
#2 Los Feliz Drive
Phillips Ranch, CA 91766
Phone: (714) 865-0175
Fax: (714) 865-3097
Contact: Patty Carpenter

Speakers Bureau Unlimited
24195 Juanita Drive
Quail Valley, CA 92587
Phone: (909) 244-6228
Fax: (909) 244-5466
Contact: Deborah Lily

AME Enterprise Bureau
7034-246 Camino Degrazia
San Diego, CA 92111
Phone: (619) 576-8047
Fax: (619) 277-9654
Contact: Ann Westrope

C.E. Seminars
2727 Camino Del Rio South, #156
San Diego, CA 92108
Phone: (619) 298-2001
Fax: (619) 688-0728
Contact: Connie Whitney

Kingbury Bureau and Management
12625 High Bluff Drive, #203
San Diego, CA 92130
Phone: (619) 481-3322
Fax: (619) 481-0422
Contact: Gail Kingsbury

Speak, Inc.
6540 Lusk Blvd., Suite 262
San Diego, CA 92121
Phone: (619) 457-9880
Fax: (619) 457-9883
Contact: Ruth Levine

Standing Ovations
8380 Miramar Mall, #225
San Diego, CA 92121
Phone: (619) 455-1850
Fax: (619) 455-1576
Contact: Nan Pratt

Santa Barbara Speakers Bureau
P.O. Box 30768
Santa Barbara, CA 93130-0768
Phone: (805) 682-7474
Fax: (805) 563-1028
Contact: Michael Pomije

Van de Walkers Speakers Bureau
104 E. Padre Street
Santa Barbara, CA 93104
Phone: (805) 687-6168
Contact: Kevin Van de Walker

Kendig Speakers Network
711 Fair Oaks Avenue, #F, Suite 160
South Pasadena, CA 91030
Phone: (818) 281-3554
Fax: (818) 281-6566
Contact: Karen Kendig

Speakers of Distinction
380 Stevens Avenue, #310
Solana Beach, CA 92075-2065
Phone: (619) 481-2977
Fax: (619) 481-2445
Contact: Donna Chyler

The Speaker Link
Box 18266
Boulder, CO 80308
Phone: (303) 494-3800/469-7333
Contact: Alison Scott

Larkin Bureau
211 Stratford Lane
Colorado Springs, CO 80909
Phone: (719) 380-9909
Fax: (719) 380-9833
Contact: Tom Larkin

Rocky Mountain Speakers Bureau
8200 S. Quebec Street A3, Suite 266
Englewood, CO 80112
Phone: (303) 792-2277
Fax: (303) 792-2278
Contact: Sharon Thayer

**Susan Miller and Associates
Speakers Bureau**
7 Red Fox Lane
Englewood, CO 80111
Phone: (303) 741-0483
Contact: Maurine Brooks

Goodman Speakers Bureau, Inc.
56 Arbor Street
Hartford, CT 06106
Phone: (203) 233-0460
Fax: (203) 236-6674
Contact: Diane Goodman

Dammah Productions
Box 254
New London, CT 06320
Phone: (203) 443-4278
Fax: (203) 444-0759
Contact: Muwwakkil Al-uqdah

The Speaker's Corner
152 Tuckahoe Drive
Shelton, CT 06484
Phone: (203) 929-4295
Fax: (203) 641-8977
Contact: David Baudoin

Educators Network
P.O. Box 953
Southport, CT 06490
Phone: (203) 254-7068
Fax: (203) 254-7027
Contact: Ann Ives

Listen Live Speaker Service
171 Hardesty Road
Stamford, CT 06903
Phone: (203) 329-9879
Contact: Jennifer Lapine

The Motivators
302 Wilton Road
Westport, CT 06880
Phone: (203) 454-7203
         (800) 237-7203
Fax: (203) 454-3241
Contact: Judith Rovins

Capital Speakers Incorporated
655 National Press Building
Washington, DC 20045
Phone: (202) 393-0772/393-1418
Contact: Phyllis McKenzie

Justice Speakers Bureau
P.O. Box 17500
Washington, DC 20041-0500
Phone: (703) 478-0100
Fax: (703) 478-0452
Contact: Jan Kary

Leading Authorities
1331 Pennsylvania Avenue, NW, #905N
Washington, DC 20004
Phone: (202) 783-0300
Fax: (202) 783-0301
Contact: Paige Darden
         Mark D. French

National Speakers Forum
5028 Wisconsin Avenue, NW, #301
Washington, DC 20016
Phone: (202) 244-1789
Fax: (202) 244-1410
Contact: Mary Sasser

Speakers Unlimited Inc.
733 15th Street, NW, Suite 510
Washington, DC 20005
Phone: (202) 783-0955
Contact: Barbara Schmidt Vance

Speakers Worldwide, Inc.
1090 Vermont Avenue, NW, Suite 300
Washington, DC 20005
Phone: (202) 408-0460
Fax: (202) 789-2279
Contact: Janet L. Cosby

Greater Orlando Speakers Bureau
Box 12353
Brooksville, FL 34601
Phone: (904) 799-6600
Contact: Sandra Baker

International Training Bureau, Inc.
Park Square
2105 Park Avenue, Suite #1
Orange Park, FL 32073
Phone: (904) 264-0897
Contact: Bob Kenny

**Accolades International
Speakers Bureau**
820 E. Highway 434, #120
Longwood, FL 32750
Phone: (407) 332-0600
Fax: (407) 332-0438
Contact: Christine and Gary Kersey

Bureau of Speakers and Seminars
P.O. Box 37
Maitland, FL 32751
Phone: (407) 647-3952
Contact: James Arch

Creative Meeting Consultants
1640 SW 84th Avenue
Miami, FL 33155
Phone: (305) 264-7780
Fax: (305) 264-0701
Contact: Loni Katine

D.M.B. Bureau
7800 Red Road, #211
Miami, FL 33143
Phone: (305) 662-9190
Contact: Dee Berkowitz

**Superstars, Speaker
Resource Bureau**
P.O. Box 2482
Orange Park, FL 32067-2482
Phone: (904) 264-1515
Contact: Ray Mack

American Speakers Bureau
5595 T. G. Lee Boulevard, Suite 178
Orlando, FL 32822
Phone: (407) 826-4248
Contact: Frank Candy

Leaders Enterprises Bureau
1 Dupont Center
390 N. Orange Avenue, #2600
Orlando, FL 32801
Phone: (407) 425-4900
Fax: (407) 422-7096
Contact: Susan Andreone

International Trainers and Speakers
200 Executive Drive
Ponte Vedra Beach, FL 32082
Phone: (904) 249-1768
Contact: Ken Taylor

Quality for Less, Inc.
8351 Roswell Road, #363
Atlanta, GA 30350
Phone: (404) 266-9088
Fax: (404) 266-9090
Contact: David Schlueter

**Resource Management
Consultants, Inc.**
5098 Vernon Springs Drive
Atlanta, GA 30338-4666
Phone: (404) 392-9174
Contact: Bernard Marino

SpeakerConnect USA
2859 Paces Ferry Road, #1920
Atlanta, GA 30339
Phone: (404) 432-1394
Fax: (404) 432-3528
Contact: Sherry Conner

The Mescon Group
One Peachtree Center, Suite 1620
Atlanta, GA 30308
Phone: (404) 656-1929
Fax: (404) 656-1926
Contact: Claire Carter

**Automation Marketing
Speakers Bureau**
640 Hoyt King Road
Bethlehem, GA 30620
Phone: (404) 867-2847
Fax: (404) 867-2563
Contact: Mark Coleman

Voice Communication Network
3050 Shallowford Road, #220
Chamblee, GA 30341
Phone: (404) 896-1854
Fax: (404) 896-1845

Madden and Associates
4955 Sherifield Drive
Marietta, GA 30067
Phone: (404) 998-7442
Contact: Debbie Madden Barnes

Convention Consultants
117 W. Perry
Savannah, GA 31401
Phone: (912) 234-4088
Contact: Maryann Smith

**Training and Speaking
Resources**
2413 Grand Avenue
Des Moines, IA 50312
Phone: (515) 244-3176
Contact: Norm Fleming

Winners Circle
6602 LaFayette Road, #130
Waterloo, IA 50701
Phone: (319) 236-9030
Fax: (319) 236-1515
Contact: Carol Van Brocklin

Universal Speakers Bureau
304 W. Hill Street
Champaign, IL 61820
Phone: (217) 333-8342
Contact: Lynne B. Hellmer

Chicago Speakers Bureau
414 N. Orleans Plaza, Suite 600
Chicago, IL 60610
Phone: (312) 661-0653
Fax: (312) 661-0622
Contact: Kathleen Sneckenberg, V.P.

Corporate Event Services
2650 Lakeview, Suite A2908
Chicago, IL 60614
Phone: (312) 975-9141
Contact: Ava Newburger

On the Scene
54 W. Illinois, #1250
Chicago, IL 60610-4305
Phone: (312) 661-1440
Fax: (312) 661-1182
Contact: Eleanor Woods

Buy Speakers Bureau
5711 W. 128th Street, Suite 13
Crestwood, IL 60445
Phone: (708) 385-5803
Contact: Douglas Buy

Multi-Cultural Speakers' Bureau
P.O. Box 7292
Elgin, IL 60121
Phone: (708) 931-9076
Contact: Arron Vessup

Motivation Media, Inc.
1245 Milwaukee Avenue
Glenview, IL 60025
Phone: (708) 297-4740
Fax: (708) 297-6829
Contact: Linda Peterson

All Occasion Speakers Bureau
6441 S. Quincy Drive
Hinsdale, IL 50532
Phone: (708) 323-3565
Contact: George O'Hare

National Speakers Bureau
222 Wisconsin Avenue
Lake Forest, IL 60045
Phone: (800) 323-9442
         (708) 295-1122
Fax: (708) 295-5292
Contact: John Palmer

Speakers International, Inc.
3316 RFD
Long Grove, IL 60047
Phone: (708) 726-0444
Contact: Cheryl Miller

NBM Bureau
1 Diversitch Drive
Manteno, IL 60950
Phone: (815) 468-3443
Fax: (815) 468-3731
Contact: Charles Betterton

Joan B. Hall and Associates
2904 Scottlynne Drive
Park Ridge, IL 60068
Phone: (708) 825-2501
Fax: (708) 291-0115
Contact: Joan Hall

Capital City Speakers Bureau
1620 S. 5th Street
Springfield, IL 62703
Phone: (217) 544-6564
Fax: (217) 544-6570
Contact: Michael T. Klemm

IEB—International Entertainment Bureau
3612 N. Washington Boulevard
Indianapolis, IN 46205-3592
Phone: (317) 926-7566
Contact: David Leonards

Indianapolis Speakers Bureau
401 Pennsylvania Parkway
Indianapolis, IN 46280-1385
Phone: (317) 848-5400
Contact: Tony Shouse

Speakers and Seminar Resources, Inc.
9220 N. College Avenue
Indianapolis, IN 46240
Phone: (317) 844-6869
Contact: Dennis E. Horvath

Five Star Speakers, Trainers and Consultants
8685 W. 96th Street
Overland Park, KS 66212
Phone: (913) 648-6480
Fax: (913) 648-6484
Contact: Nancy Lauterbach

North American Speakers Bureau
6701 W. 64th Street, #100
Overland Park, KS 66202
Phone: (913) 677-1444
Fax: (913) 677-1805
Contact: Brad Plumb

Fielder Group Speakers Bureau
Route 2, Box 372
Gilbertsville, KY 42022
Phone: (502) 362-7129
Fax: (502) 362-7130
Contact: Barbara Fielder

Program Resources
P.O. Box 22307
Louisville, KY 40252
Phone: (502) 339-1653
Contact: Madolyn Wright

Star Productions Speakers Bureau
4123 Worthy Drive
Lake Charles, LA 70605
Phone: (318) 479-1230
Contact: Robert Beam

Simply Speaking
414 Brockenbraugh Court
Metairie, LA 70005
Phone: (800) 299-6338
         (504) 838-3051
Contact: Carolyn and Reginald
         Sanders

American Program Bureau
36 Crafts Street
Newton, MA 02158
Phone: (617) 965-6600
Fax: (617) 965-6610
Contact: Perry Steinberg, CEO

Speakers Guild
78 Old King's Highway
Sandwich, MA 02563
Phone: (508) 888-6702
Fax: (508) 888-6771
Contact: Ed Larkin

Patton Consultant Services
650 Asbury Street
South Hamilton, MA 01982
Phone: (508) 468-3720
Fax: (508) 468-7604
Contact: Nancy Palmer

Excellan Bureau
1251 W. Montgomery Avenue,
Room 351
Rockville, MD 20850
Phone: (703) 242-2448
Contact: Judy Doe/Parker Rogers

Podium Professionals
P.O. Box 3410
Ann Arbor, MI 48106
Phone: (313) 663-5080
Fax: (313) 662-8820
Contact: Vicki Niebrugge

Educators Job Connection
5859 Winans Drive
Brighton, MI 48116
Phone: (313) 231-9442
Contact: Jeannine Cronkhite

Bernie Stevens and Associates
747 W. Maple, Suite 501
Clawson, MI 48017
Phone: (313) 288-0338
          (800) FOR BERNIE

Michigan Speakers Bureau
33117 Hamilton Ct., #100
Farmington Hills, MI 48018
Phone: (313) 489-5771
Contact: Dee Lynn

Network Productions, Inc.
161 Ottawa, NW
107E Waters Building
Grand Rapids, MI 49503
Phone: (800) 669-RSVP
          (616) 235-0777
Fax: (616) 235-0743
Contact: Robert W. Barss

Master Marketing Corp.
2180 Grenadier
Troy, MI 48098
Phone: (313) 689-6650
Fax: (313) 853-2495
Contact: Bob Mohr

YES...A Positive Network
2690 Croks Road, Suite 116
Troy, MI 48084
Phone: (313) 362-2424
Fax: (313) 362-2741
Contact: Michael Jeffreys

**Motivational Speakers
and Entertainment**
14055 Grand Avenue South, Suite E
Burnsville, MN 55337
Phone: (612) 898-4022
Fax: (612) 898-4022
Contact: Cindy Griefe Chapman

The Speakers Bureau, Inc.
9456 Club House Road
Eden Prairie, MN 55347
Phone: (612) 942-6768
Fax: (612) 941-1994
Contact: Renee Strom

Preferred Speakers
7200 France Avenue S., #336
Minneapolis, MN 55435-4310
Phone: (612) 831-5039
Fax: (612) 831-4607
Contact: Warren and Sheila Burke
          Tom Cavanaugh

Speakers USA
2221 Minneapolis Avenue
Minneapolis, MN 55406
Phone: (612) 338-8805
Contact: Al Porte

Professional Development Associates
31020 County Road 2
St. Joseph, MN 56374
Phone: (612) 363-4555
Contact: Jeanie Wilkens

Celebrity Plus, Inc.
55 Maryland Plaza
St. Louis, MO 63108
Phone: (314) 367-5588
Fax: (314) 367-5599
Contact: Lisa Butts

Caves & Associates
Trainers and Speakers Bureau
219 Highland Village
Jackson, MS 39211
Phone: (601) 981-9834
Fax: (601) 981-8150
Contact: Roy Caves

Speakers Network
Box 15219
2727 Rothwood Drive
Charlotte, NC 28211
Phone: (704) 364-7461
Fax: (704) 364-4981
Contact: Sandra Roork

Speakers and More
P.O. Box 33784
Raleigh, NC 27636
Phone: (919) 851-9192
Fax: (919) 851-9038
Contact: Marie Long

Medical Speakers International
Box 14381
Research Triangle Park, NC 27709
Phone: (919) 361-2940
Fax: (919) 361-0410
Contact: Julia Barnes Oliver

ICAN Bureau
2120 S. 72nd Street, #1052
Omaha, NE 68106
Phone: (402) 392-0746
Contact: Fran Root

Shirley Hoe Enterprises
142 Hillside Avenue
Berkeley Heights, NJ 07922
Phone: (908) 464-2844
Contact: Shirley Hoe

First Choice Bureau
10-A Toledo Tower
Cherry Hill, NJ 08002
Phone: (609) 482-1474
Fax: (609) 667-4984
Contact: Doug Heir

NLK Enterprises
Box 4422
Clifton, NJ 07012
Phone: (201) 779-2455
Contact: Mary Kaplus

Ridings Resource Group Ltd.
235 Martha Avenue
Elmwood Park, NJ 07407-1135
Phone: (201) 843-6370
       (717) 898-9247
Fax: (717) 392-7500
Contact: Phillip Alotta

JR Associates—Meetings,
Conventions and Speakers
86 Poe Road
Princeton, NJ 08540
Phone: (609) 921-6605
Fax: (609) 921-6960
Contact: Janet Pickover

Eagles Talent Associates, Inc.
P.O. Box 859
Short Hills, NJ 07078-0859
Phone: (201) 376-3737
Fax: (201) 376-3660
Contact: Esther Eagles

Leigh Bureau
50 Division Street, #200
Somerville, NJ 08876-2955
Phone: (908) 253-8600
Fax: (908) 253-8601
Contact: Larry Leson
        Daniel Stern

P.D.O. Info-Sources
P.O. Box 286
Cochiti Lake, NM 87083
Phone: (505) 465-2806
Fax: (505) 465-2806
Contact: Paul Oyer

Provoices Speakers Bureau
P.O. Box 13309, University Street
Reno, NV 89507-3309
Phone: (702) 345-0340
Contact: Tom Kubistant

Capital Speakers Bureau
12 Prospect Terrace
Albany, NY 12208
Phone: (518) 489-7825
Fax: (518) 489-3533
Contact: Audrey Hoffman

Arnesen Speakers Bureau
765 Dodge Road
Getzville, NY 14068
Phone: (716) 689-1686
Contact: Bernie Arnesen

L & G, Inc. (Harrison Corp.)
Lattingtown Road
Glen Cove, NY 11542
Phone: (516) 671-9500
Contact: Lola Green

**Management Training
and Consulting**
524 Latham Road
Mineola, NY 11501
Phone: (516) 248-3820
Fax: (516) 746-1474
Contact: Rich Keegan

Westvale Talent Bureau
600 C. Pelham Road
New Rochelle, NY 10805
Phone: (914) 633-9227
Contact: Randall Ehman

**Bendel and Associates
Speakers Bureau**
220 Fifth Avenue, 3rd Floor
New York, NY 10001
Phone: (212) 725-0707
Fax: (212) 725-2254
Contact: Margo Black

Greater Talent Network
150 5th Avenue
New York, NY 10011
Phone: (212) 645-4200
Fax: (212) 627-1471
Contact: Don R. Epstein

Harry Walker Agency, Inc.
One Penn Plaza, Suite 2400
New York, NY 10119
Phone: (212) 563-0700
Fax: (212) 629-7958
Contact: Don Walker

ICM Artists, Ltd.
40 West 57th Street
New York, NY 10019
Phone: (212) 556-5600
Fax: (212) 556-5677
Contact: Jim Jermanok

Master Media Ltd. and Baumann
16 E. 72nd Street
New York, NY 10021-4126
Phone: (212) 246-9500
Contact: Phyllis Parrish

MFA Communications
825 Eighth Avenue
New York, NY 10019
Phone: (212) 474-5483
Contact: Maryann Flanagan

New York Speakers Bureau
10 Jones Street, #6K
New York, NY 10014-5650
Phone: (212) 353-8640
Contact: Rodger McFarlane

Results Unlimited
Box 1020
New York, NY 10028
Phone: (212) 734-3103
Contact: Helen Trautman

Smart Luck, Inc.
875 Park Avenue
New York, NY 10021
Phone: (212) 628-8731
Contact: Gail Howard

Speakers Plus
245 W. 19th Street
New York, NY 10011
Phone: (212) 929-6776
Fax: (212) 242-3968
Contact: Sue Broslaw

Twenty First Century Associates
2 East 37th Street
New York, NY 10016
Phone: (212) 447-7030
Fax: (212) 725-3972
Contact: Alisa Swarts

Bentley-Hall, Inc.
120 Walton Street, Suite 201
Syracuse, NY 13302-1211
Phone: (315) 422-4488
Fax: (315) 422-3837
Contact: Bob Popyk

Metro Speakers Bureau
5 Woodthrush Drive
West Nyack, NY 10994
Phone: (914) 357-3403
Contact: Susan Halfon

Program Corporation of America
599 W. Hartsdale Avenue
White Plains, NY 10607
Phone: (914) 428-5840
Fax: (914) 428-5356
Contact: Alan Walker

Scipio Bureau
1501 E. 191 Street, #407
Cleveland, OH 44117
Phone: (216) 692-3176
Contact: Beverly Scipio

Speakers Unlimited
Box 27225
Columbus, OH 43227
Phone: (614) 864-3703/864-3753
Fax: (614) 864-3876
Contact: D. Michael Frank

SRM Leader Bureau
1580 Alton Darby Cr. Road
Columbus, OH 43228
Phone: (614) 878-1023
Contact: Geneva Mossa

**Command Performance
Speakers Bureau**
1601 W. Okmulgee Avenue, #2000
Muskogee, OK 74401
Phone: (918) 687-3385
Contact: Sharon B. Thomas

**Good Entertainment
and Speakers Bureau**
1105 NW 63rd
Oklahoma City, OK 73116
Phone: (405) 840-2020
Fax: (405) 842-5451
Contact: Gary Good

Tulsa Impact Unlimited
3010 S. Harvard
Harvard Building, #330
Tulsa, OK 74105
Phone: (918) 749-1749
Fax: (918) 743-8451
Contact: Karen Eycleshymer
        Barbara Maxwell

R & R Speakers Bureau
Box 896
Ashland, OR 97520
Phone: (503) 488-2992
Fax: (503) 488-2992
Contact: Lindea Bowe Kirchner

Northwest Speakers Connection
425 NW 18th Avenue, #5
Portland, OR 97209-2229
Phone: (503) 228-1528
Fax: (503) 228-1521
Contact: Larry Cavender

Read Speakers and Trainers Bureau
6446 N.E. 30
Portland, OR 97211
Phone: (503)281-2569
Contact: Francine Read

Future Consultants Bureau
105 B West Ashland Street
Doylestown, PA 18901
Phone: (215) 340-0534
Contact: Bill Tomaszewski

Speaker Services
765 Ormond Avenue
Drexel Hill, PA 19026
Phone: (215) 626-4600
Fax: (215) 626-6688
Contact: William D. Thompson

Showcase Associates, Inc.
911 Cypress Avenue
Elkins Park, PA 19117
Phone: (215) 884-6205
Contact: Carole Howey

Dr. Dooley Speakers Bureau
7020 Frankford Avenue
Philadelphia, PA 19135
Phone: (215) 331-2202
Contact: Dr. Richard J. Dooley

Motivation Unlimited Bureau
223 Sheldon Avenue
Pittsburgh, PA 15220
Phone: (412) 276-1885
Contact: Dick Reibel

Results Unlimited
421 Cochran Road, #205
Pittsburgh, PA 15228
Phone: (412) 344-7477
Contact: Helen Trautman

Rodgers Enterprises
P.O. Box 5805
Charleston, SC 29406-0805
Phone: (803) 863-0441
Contact: B.J. Rodgers

Blakemore & Dunn Speakers Bureau
P.O. Box 8858
Columbia, SC 29202
Phone: (803) 796-1965
Contact: Carol Waldo

Sylvester Management Corp.
P.O. Box 986
Irmo, SC 29063
Phone: (803) 781-1638
Contact: Ted Hamre

Speakers Plus, Inc.
3209 Hall Street
Rapid City, SD 55435-5113
Phone: (605) 348-5586
Fax: (605) 348-1448
Contact: Patricia Pummel

Strictly Speaking
Box 89604
Sioux Falls, SD 56105
Phone: (605) 334-1105
Contact: Terry Dickman

Executive Speakers Bureau
8843 Bazemore Road
Cordova, TN 38018
Phone: (901) 754-9404
Fax: (901) 748-1431
Contact: Sudoth Schelp

Happy Talk Speaking Services
1003 Heritage Village
Madison, TN 37155
Phone: (615) 865-2041
Fax: (615) 865-2041
Contact: Peggy and George Goldtrap

Management Seminars, Inc.
P.O. Box 240204
Memphis, TN 38124
Phone: (901) 767-2408
Contact: Ann Simon

Ambassador Artists Agency
P.O. Box 50358
Nashville, TN 37205
Phone: (615) 352-3291
Fax: (615) 352-3292
Contact: Wes Yode

Resource Group of America, Inc.
P.O. Box 140430
Nashville, TN 37214
Phone: (615) 889-4676
Fax: (615) 889-4448
Contact: Charles W. Whitnel, Jr.

Top Billing International
Box 121089
Nashville, TN 37219
Phone: (615) 327-1133
Contact: Tandy Rice

International Speakers Network
Box 4189
Sevierville, TN 37864-9906
Phone: (800) 728-0253
Fax: (615) 429-4523
Contact: David Wright

Hispanic Speakers Unlimited
16712 Rivendell Lane
Austin, TX 78737
Phone: (512) 858-4623
Contact: Patricia Obeso Olquin

Speaker & Celebrity Agency
1816 Treeline Drive
Carrollton, TX 75007
Phone: (214) 394-7013
Fax: (214) 492-3767
Contact: Gayle Cowger

Zig Ziglar—Speakers Bureau
3330 Earheart St., Suite 204
Carrollton, TX 75006-5026
Phone: (214) 233-9191
Contact: Bryan Flanagan

Grabow Bureau
16775 Addison Road, Suite #630
Dallas, TX 75248
Phone: (214) 250-1162
Contact: C.J. Polk
        Director of Marketing

Incredible Productions
3327 Wyli
Dallas, TX 75235
Phone: (214) 350-3633
Contact: Mark Martin

Joan Frank Productions
8175 Clearsprings Road
Dallas, TX 75240
Phone: (214) 470-9500
Contact: Brad Lee

Speaker's College
7278 Alto Carro
Dallas, TX 75248
Phone: (214) 994-7719
Contact: Randy Marshall, Ph.D.

Speaker's Source International
P.O. Box 741414
Dallas, TX 75374-1414
Phone: (214) 783-9111
Fax: (214) 783-9111
Contact: Linkie Seltzer

TRB Speakers Bureau
14902 Preston Road, #212, Suite 184
Dallas, TX 75240
Phone: (214) 233-3282
Contact: Pat Roper

Verbal Communications
12700 Preston Road, #170
Dallas, TX 75230
Phone: (214) 387-3743
Contact: Gloria Hoffman

American Speakers Association
P.O. Box 6925
Houston, TX 77265
Phone: (713) 665-1736
Fax: (713) 661-2331
Contact: Carol Posey

Creative Speech Interests
4770 W. Belfort, #111
Houston, TX 77035
Phone: (713) 627-7960
Contact: Marjorie Best

Training Network
2537 S. Gessner, Suite 109
Houston, TX 77063
Phone: (713) 784-3405
Contact: Sherry Lewis

Corporate Educational Resources
6309 N. O'Connor, #215
Irving, TX 75039-3510
Phone: (214) 506-9988
Contact: Susan Parker

Garrett Speakers International, Inc.
3401 W. Airport Fwy.,
Suite 106–133
Irving, TX 75062
Phone: (214) 513-0054
Fax: (214) 513-0540
Contact: Betty and Gene Garrett

Winner's Circle—A Speaker's Bureau
12 Inwood Manor
San Antonio, TX 78248
Phone: (210) 492-4249
Fax: (210) 492-4249
Contact: Jack Warkenthien

WRS Speakers Bureau
Box 21207
Waco, TX 76702-1207
Phone: (800) 299-3366
Fax: (817) 757-1454
Contact: Ingrid Harding

Darick Motivational Resources Speakers Bureau
Box 1444
Salt Lake City, UT 84110
Phone: (801) A-MOTIVE
Fax: (801) 254-5871
Contact: Darol Wagstaff

C.C. & L. Speakers Group, Inc.
1320 Old Chain Bridge Road, #360
McLean, VA 22101
Phone: (703) 734-2344
Contact: Joseph Cosby

Speakers Plus
316 Tabbs Lane
Newport News, VA 23602
Phone: (800) 225-2338
Contact: Wanda Watson

Washington Speakers Bureau
310 S. Henry Street
Old Town Alexandria, VA 22314
Phone: (703) 684-0555
Fax: (703) 684-9378
Contact: Bernie Swain

Success Library Speakers Bureau
Box 2402
Virginia Beach, VA 23450
Phone: (804) 431-1325
Contact: Virginia Grugett

Brown Bag Plus Bureau
2133 E. Interlaken Boulevard, #1
Seattle, WA 98112
Phone: (206) 329-3095
Contact: Margarite Peterson

C.B.C.S. Ltd.
P.O. Box 4202
Seattle, WA 98104
Phone: (206) 624-5501
Fax: (206) 932-6816
Contact: Charlotte Benson

George Carlson & Associates
Western Lecture/Entertainment
2512 Second Avenue, #306
Seattle, WA 98121
Phone: (206) 441-1466
Contact: George Carlson

University of Washington
Speakers Bureau
4014 University Way NE
Seattle, WA 98105
Phone: (206) 543-9198
Fax: (206) 543-0786
Contact: Kevin Henry

Portland Speakers Bureau
703 Broadway Street, #500
Vancouver, WA 98660-3306
Phone: (503) 241-2411
Fax: (503) 693-6121
Contact: Carly Holiday

Associated Speakers, Inc.
12700 W. Bluemound Road
Elm Grove, WI 53122
Phone: (414) 782-9020
Fax: (414) 782-4759
Contact: Jerald Reckner

Abbott-Jeffers and Associates
Box 331
Iola, WI 54945
Phone: (715) 445-3525
Contact: Bob Lord

Speakers Mart
7117 Turnberry Road
Madison, WI 53719
Phone: (608) 274-3271
Contact: Lorell Bruce

Great Ideas! Speakers Bureau
and Meeting Planner
2437 N. Booth Street
Milwaukee, WI 53212
Phone: (414) 374-5433
Contact: Patricia Clasen

Cruise Line Bureaus

Creative Cruises Exclusively
35736 Dearing
Sterling Heights, MI 48312
Phone: (313) 268-6500
(800) 882-2299
Fax: (313) 268-0026
Contact: Peg Ostby

Lecturers International
Box 35446
Tucson, AZ 85704
Phone: (602) 297-1145
Fax: (602) 297-2324
Contact: Helen Kelly

POSH Talks
Box 2829
Palm Desert, CA 92261
Phone: (619) 340-3117
Contact: Lenore McHenry

Program Experts Inc.
Box 510
Cresskill, NJ 07626-0510
Phone: (201) 569-7950
Fax: (201) 569-8740
Contact: Joann Osoff

Royal Cruise Lines
Phone: (800) 622-0538 (California)
(800) 227-5628
Contact: Patricia Roberts

Working Vacation
4277 Lake Santa Clara Drive
Santa Clara, CA 95054-1330
Phone: (408) 727-9665
Contact: Lauretta Blake

National Seminar Sites for Financial Seminars

Here is a list of quality seminar sites throughout the United States. These sites are especially appropriate for financial seminars.

ARIZONA

Phoenix

Arizona Biltmore
24th Street and Missouri, 85016
(602) 954-2523

Boulders Resort
34631 N. Tom Darlington Drive
Carefree, 85377
(602) 488-9009, (800) 553-1717

Crescent Koll Center
2620 W. Dunlap Avenue, 85021
(602) 943-8200, (800) 423-4216

Embassy Suites Biltmore
2630 E. Camelback Road, 85016
(602) 955-3992, (800) 362-2779

Fountains Suite Hotel
2577 W. Greenway Road, 85023
(602) 375-1777, (800) 338-1338

Holiday Inn Corporate Center
2532 W. Peoria Avenue, 85029
(602) 943-2341, (800) 843-3663

Hyatt Regency
122 N. 2nd Street, 85004
(602) 252-1234, (800) 228-9000

Pointe Hilton at Squaw Peak
7677 N. 16th Street, 85020
(602) 997-2626

Ritz-Carlton Phoenix
2401 E. Camelback Road, 85016
(602) 468-0793

Sheraton San Marco Golf and Conference Center
One San Marcos Place, 85224
(602) 963-6655, (800) 528-8071

Westcourt Hotel
10220 N. Metro Parkway East, 85051
(602) 997-5900, (800) 858-1033

CALIFORNIA

Anaheim

Anaheim Inn at the Park
1855 S. Harbor Boulevard, 92802
(714) 971-3626, (800) 421-6662

Crown Sterling Suites
3100 E. Frontera, 92806
(800) 433-4600

Disneyland Hotel
1150 W. Cerritos Avenue, 92802
(714) 956-6510

Hilton and Towers Anaheim
777 Convention Way, 92802-3497
(714) 740-4220, (800) 445-8667

Bel Air

Bel Air Summit
11461 Sunset Boulevard, 90049-2099
(213) 476-6571, (800) 333-3333

Beverly Hills

Beverly Hills Hotel
9641 Sunset Boulevard, 90210
(310) 276-2251, (800) 283-8885

Hilton Beverly
9876 Wilshire Boulevard, 90210
(310) 274-7777, (800) 445-8667

L'Ermitage
9291 Burton Way, 90210
(310) 278-3344, (800) 800-2113

Radisson Beverly Pavilion Hotel
9360 Wilshire Boulevard, 90210
(310) 273-1400, (800) 441-5050

The Regent Beverly Wilshire
9500 Wilshire Boulevard, 90212
(310) 275-5200, (800) 545-4000

Century City

**Westin Century Plaza Hotel
and Tower**
2025 Avenue of the Stars, 90067
(310) 551-3342, (800) 228-3000

**J.W. Marriott Hotel
at Century City**
2151 Avenue of the Stars, 90067
(310) 277-2777, (800) 228-9290

City of Commerce

Radisson Hotel City of Commerce
6300 E. Telegraph Road, 90040
(213)722-7200, (800) 333-3333

City of Industry

Sheraton Resort Industry Hills
One Industry Hills Parkway, 91744
(818) 754-2416, (800) 325-3535

Hollywood

Beverly Garland's Holiday Inn
4222 Vineland Avenue
N. Hollywood, 91602
(818) 980-8000, (800) BEVERLY

Hyatt on Sunset
8401 Sunset Boulevard, 90069
(213) 656-4101, (800) 228-9000

Roosevelt Hotel Hollywood
7000 Hollywood Boulevard, 90028
(213) 466-7000, (800) 950-766

Los Angeles

The Biltmore
506 S. Grand Avenue, 90071-2607
(213) 624-1011, (800) 245-8673

Century Plaza Hotel and Tower
2025 Avenue of the Stars, 90067
(310) 277-2000, (800) 228-3000

Hilton and Towers Los Angeles
930 Wilshire Boulevard, 90017
(213) 629-4321, (800) 445-8667

Holiday Inn Brentwood
170 N. Church Lane, 90049
(310) 476-6411, (800) HOLIDAY

Hyatt Regency Los Angeles
711 South Hope Street, 90017
(213) 683-1234, (800) 233-1234

New Otani Hotel and Gardens
120 S. Los Angeles Street, 90012
(213) 629-1200, (800) 421-8795

Radisson Wilshire Plaza
3515 Wilshire Boulevard, 90010
(213) 368-3003

Sheraton Grande Los Angeles
333 S. Figueroa Street, 90071
(213) 617-1133

UCLA Conference and Event Management
330 DeNeve Drive, 90024-1492
(310) 825-5305

Westin Bonaventure
404 S. Figueroa Street, 90071
(213) 624-1000, (800) 228-3000

San Diego

Bahia Hotel
998 W. Mission Bay Drive, 92109
(619) 488-0551, (800) 288-0770

Hilton Beach and Tennis Resort
1775 E. Mission Bay Drive, 92109
(619) 276-4010, (800) HILTONS

Hotel Del Coronado
1500 Orange Avenue
Coronado, 92118
(619) 522-8000

Hyatt Regency San Diego
1 Market Place
San Diego, 92101
(619) 687-6040, (800) 233-1234

Marriott Hotel and Marina
333 W. Harbor Drive, 92101
(619) 234-1500

Pan Pacific San Diego
400 W. Broadway, 92101
(619) 239-4527

Rancho Bernardo Inn
17550 Bernardo Oaks Drive, 92128
(619) 487-1611, (800) 854-1065

San Diego Princess Resort
1404 W. Vacation Road, 92109
(619) 581-5900, (800) 542-6275

Sheraton Harbor Island Hotel
1380 Harbor Island Drive, 92101
(619) 692-2200, (800) 325-3535

U.S. Grant
326 Broadway, 92101
(619) 232-3121, (800) 854-2608

Westgate Hotel
1055 Second Avenue, 92101
(619) 238-1818, (800) 221-3802

San Francisco

Campton Place
Stockton Street, 94108
(415) 781-5555, (800) 426-3135

Donatello
501 Post Street, 94102
(415) 885-8810, (800) 227-3184

Fairmont Hotel and Tower
Nob Hill, 94106
(415) 772-5000, (800) 527-4727

Four Seasons Clift Hotel
495 Geary Street, 94102
(415) 775-4700, (800) 332-3442

Grand Hyatt San Francisco
345 Stockton, 94108
(415) 398-1234, (800) 233-1234

Handlery Union Square Hotel
351 Geary Street, 94102
(415) 781-7800, (800) 843-4343

Hilton and Towers San Francisco
333 O'Farrell Street, 94102
(415) 771-1400, (800)-HILTONS

Holiday Inn Civic Center
50 8th Street, 94103
(415) 626-6103, (800) 465-4329

Mark Hopkins Inter-Continental
One Nob Hill, 94108
(415) 392-3434, (800) 327-0200

Marriott San Francisco
55 4th Street, 94103
(415) 896-1600, (800) 228-9290

Mikayo Hotel
1625 Post Street, 94115
(415) 922-3200, (800) 533-4567

Nikko San Francisco
222 Mason Street, 94102
(415) 394-1111, (800) 645-5687

Parc Fifty Five Hotel
55 Cyril Magnin Street, 94102-2865
(415) 392-8000, (800) 650-7272

Ritz Carlton
600 Stockton at California, 94108
(415) 296-7465, (800) 241-3333

Sheraton at Fisherman's Wharf
2500 Mason Street, 94133
(415) 363-5500, (800) 325-3535

Sir Francis Drake
450 Powell Street, 94102
(415) 392-7755, (800) 227-5480

Stouffer Stanford Court Hotel
905 California Street, 94108
(415) 989-3500, (800) 227-4736

Westin St. Francis
335 Powell Street, 94102
(415) 774-0112, (800) 228-3000

COLORADO

Denver

Brown Palace Hotel
321 17th Street, 80202
(303) 297-3111, (800) 321-2599

Doubletree Denver Southeast
13696 E. Iliff Place
Aurora, 80014
(303) 337-2800, (800) 243-3112

**Embassy Suites Hotel
Denver Southeast**
7525 E. Hampden Avenue, 80237
(303) 696-6644, (800) 525-3585

Executive Tower Inn
1405 Curtis Street, 80202
(303) 571-0300, (800) 525-6651

Holiday Inn Denver North
4849 Bannock Street, 80216
(303) 292-9500, (800)-HOLIDAY

Hyatt Regency Tech Center
7800 E. Tufts Avenue, 80237
(303) 779-1234, (800) 233-1234

Marriott Hotel Center Center
1701 California Street, 90202
(303) 297-1300, (800) 228-9290

Radisson Hotel Denver
1550 Court Place, 80202-5199
(303) 893-3333, (800) 333-3333

Registry Denver
3203 Quebec Street, 80207
(303) 321-3333

**Scantion Conference Center
Hotel and Resort**
200 Inverness Drive
W. Englewood, 80112
(303) 799-5800, (800) 346-4891

Warwick Hotel
1776 Grand Street, 80203
(303) 861-2000, (800) 525-2888

Westin Tabor Center Denver
1672 Lawrence Street, 80202
(303) 572-9100, (800) 228-3000

CONNECTICUT

Greenwich

Hyatt Regency Greenwich
1800 E. Putnam Avenue, 06870
(203) 637-1234, (800) 233-1234

Hartford

Holiday Inn Hartford
50 Morgan Street, 06120-2994
(203) 549-2400, (800) 465-4329

Sheraton Hartford
315 Trumbull Street, 06103
(203) 728-5151, (800) 325-3535

Marriott Framington
15 Farm Springs Road
Framington 06032
(203) 678-1000, (800) 228-9290

Stamford

Marriott Hotel
Two Stamford Forum, 06901
(203) 977-1285, (800) 831-1000

Radisson Tara Hotel
2701 Summer Street, 06905
(203) 359-1300, (800) 333-3333

Ramada Hotel
700 Main Street, 06901
(203) 358-8400, (800) 562-9110

Sheraton Stamford Hotel
One First Stamford Place, 06902
(203) 967-2222, (800) 325-3535

DISTRICT OF COLUMBIA

Days Inn Downtown
1201 K Street NW, 20005
(202) 842-1020, (800) 633-1414

Dupont Plaza Hotel
1500 New Hampshire Avenue NW,
20036
(202) 483-6000, (800) 421-6662

Embassy Row Hotel
2015 Massachusetts Avenue NW,
20036
(202) 265-1600, (800) 424-2400

Four Seasons Hotel
2800 Pennsylvania Avenue NW, 20007
(202) 342-0444, (800) 268-6282

**Georgetown University
Conference Center**
37th and O Streets NW, 20016
(202) 625-4763

Grand Hotel of Washington, D.C.
2350 M Street NW, 20037
(202) 429-0100, (800) 888-4747

Grand Hyatt Washington
1000 H Street NW, 20001
(202) 582-1234, (800) 223-1234

Hilton and Towers Washington
1919 Connecticut Avenue NW, 20009
(202) 483-3000, (800) 445-8667

Holiday Inn Capitol
550 C Street NW, 20024
(202) 479-4000, (800) 465-4329

Inter-Continental Willard
1401 Pennsylvania Avenue, 20004
(202) 628-9100, (800) 327-0200

Loews L'Enfant Plaza
480 L'Enfant Plaza SW, 20024
(202) 484-1000

Madison Hotel
15th and M Streets NW, 20005
(202) 862-1600, (800) 424-8577

J.W. Marriott at National Place
1331 Pennsylvania Avenue NW, 20004
(202) 393-2000, (800) 228-9290

Omni Shoreham
2500 Calvert Street NW, 20008
(202) 234-0700, (800) 843-6664

Park Hyatt Hotel
24th and M Streets NW, 20037
(202) 789-1234, (800) 922-7275

Quality Inn Capitol Hill Hotel
415 New Jersey Avenue NW, 20001
(202) 638-1616, (800) 228-5151

Radisson Park Terrace
1515 Rhode Island Avenue NW, 20005
(202) 232-7000, (800) 333-3333

Ramada Washington Plaza Hotel
10 Thomas Circle NW
Massachusetts and Vermont Avenues,
20005
(202) 842-1300, (800) 424-1140

Ritz-Carlton Hotel
2100 Massachusetts NW, 20008
(202) 293-2100, (800) 241-3333

Sheraton Washington Hotel
2660 Woodley Road NW, 20008
(202) 328-2000, (800) 325-3535

Stouffer Mayflower Hotel
1127 Connecticut Avenue NW, 20036
(202) 347-3000, (800) 468-3571

Vista International Hotel
1400 M Street NW, 20005
(202) 429-1700, (800) 847-8232

Washington D.C. Renaissance Hotel
999 Ninth Street NW, 20016
(202) 682-4041, (800) 228-9898

Watergate Hotel
2650 Virginia Avenue NW, 20037
(202) 298-4491

FLORIDA

Miami

Doral Resort and Country Club
4400 NW 87th Avenue, 33178-2192
(305) 592-2000, (800) 327-6334

Du Pont Plaza Hotel
300 Biscayne Boulevard Way, 33131
(305) 358-2541, (800) 327-3480

Holiday Inn Downtown Miami
200 SE Second Street, 33131
(305) 374-3000, (800) HOLIDAY

Howard Johnson Golden Glades
16500 NW 2nd Avenue, 33169
(305) 945-2621, (800) 654-2000

Hyatt Regency Miami
400 SW 2nd Avenue, 33131
(305) 358-1234, (800) 228-9000

Inter-Continental Hotel Miami
100 Chopin Plaza, 31331
(305) 577-1000, (800) 327-3005

**Marriott Biscayne Bay Hotel
and Marina**
1633 N. Biscayne Drive, 33132
(305) 374-3900, (800) 228-9290

Omni International Hotel Miami
1601 Biscayne Boulevard, 33132
(305) 374-0000, (800) 228-2121

Palm Bay Hotel and Club
780 NE 69th Street, 33138
(305) 757-3500, (800) 854-5636

Radisson Center
777 NW 72nd Avenue, 33126
(305) 261-2900

Sheraton Brickell Point Miami
495 Brickell Avenue, 33131
(305) 373-6000, (800) 325-3535

Turnberry Isle Resort and Club
19999 W. Country Club Drive, 33180
(305) 932-6200, (800) 233-1588

Miami Beach

Castle Beach Club
5445 Collins Avenue, 33140
(305) 865-1500, (800) 352-3224

Doral OceanBeach Resort
4833 Collins Avenue, 33140
(305) 532-3600 (800) 32-DORAL

Dilido Beach Resort Hotel
155 Lincoln Road, 33139
(305) 538-0811, (800) 327-1641

Eden Roc Resort Hotel
4525 Collins Avenue, 33140
(305) 531-0000, (800) 327-8337

Hilton Fontainebleau Resort and Spa
4441 Collins Avenue, 33140
(305) 535-3255, (800) HILTONS

Ramada Resort Deauville Hotel
6701 Collins Avenue, 33141
(305) 865-8511, (800) 327-6656

GEORGIA

Atlanta

**Castlegate Hotel
and Conference Center**
I-78 at Howell Mill Road NW, 30318
(404) 881-6000, (800) 228-9898

Colony Square Hotel
Peachtree and 14th Street, 30361
(404) 892-6000, (800) 422-7895

Doubletree Hotel at Concourse
7 Concourse Parkway, 30328
(404) 395-3900, (800) 528-0444

Embassy Suites Galleria
2815 Akers Mill Road, 30339
(404) 984-9300, (800) 362-2779

Hilton and Towers Atlanta
255 Courtland Street NE, 30303
(404) 659-2000, (800) 445-8667

Holiday Inn Buckhead
3340 Peachtree Street NE, 30026
(404) 231-1234, (800) 241-7078

Hyatt Regency at Atlanta
265 Peachtree Street NE, 30303
(404) 577-1234, (800) 223-1234

Marriott Marquis Atlanta
265 Peachtree Center Avenue NE,
30303
(404) 521-0000, (800) 228-9290

Omni Hotel and CNN Center
100 CNN Center, 30335
(404) 659-0000, (800) 843-8664

**Peachtree Executive
Conference Center**
2443 Highway 54 W.
Peachtree City, 30269
(404) 487-2000, (800) PEACH-11

Penta Hotel Atlanta
590 W. Peachtree Street NW, 30308
(404) 881-6000, (800) 633-0000

Radisson Hotel Atlanta
165 Courtland Street, 30303
(404) 659-6500, (800) 333-3333

Ritz-Carlton Atlanta
181 Peachtree Street NE, 30303
(404) 659-0400, (800) 241-3333

Sheraton Century Center Hotel
2000 Century Boulevard NE,
30345-3377
(404) 325-0000, (800) 325-3535

Stouffer Waverly Hotel
2450 Galleria Parkway, 30339
(404) 953-4500, (800) 468-3571

Swiss Hotel Atlanta
3391 Peachtree Road NE, 30326
(404) 365-0065

Travelodge Hotel Atlanta
2061 N. Druid Hills Road NE, 30329
(404) 321-4174, (800) 255-3050

Westin Lenox
3300 Lenox Road NE, 30326
(404) 262-3344, (800) 228-3000

HAWAII

Honolulu

Ala Moana Hotel
410 Atkinson Drive, 96814
(808) 955-4811, (800) 367-6025

Halekulani Hotel
2199 Kalia Road, 96815
(808) 923-2311, (800) 367-2343

Hawaiian Regent
2552 Kalakaua Avenue, 96815
(808) 922-6611, (800) 367-5121

Hilton Hawaiian Village
2005 Kalia Road, 96815
(808) 949-4321, (800) 445-8667

Hyatt Regency Waikiko
2424 Kalakaua Avenue, 96815
(808) 923-1234, (800) 923-1234

Ihilani Resort and Spa
92-1001 Olani Street
Kapolei, 96707
(808) 679-0079, (800) 626-4446

Ilikai
1777 Ala Moana Boulevard, 96815
(808) 949-3811, (800) 733-7777

Outrigger Prince Kuhio Hotel
2500 Kuhio Avenue, 96815
(808) 922-0811, (800) 733-7777

Pacific Beach Hotel
2490 Kalakaua Avenue, 96815
(808) 922-1233, (800) 367-6060

Pagoda Hotel
1525 Raycroft Street, 96814
(808) 941-6611, (800) 367-6060

Sheraton Princell Kaiulani
120 Kaiulani Avenue, 96815
(808) 922-5811

Waikiki Beachcomber Hotel
2300 Kalakaua Avenue, 96815
(808) 922-4646, (800) 622-4646

Waikiki Parc Hotel
2233 Helumoa Road, 96815
(808) 921-7272, (800) 422-0450

ILLINOIS

Chicago

Allerton Hotel
701 N. Michigan Avenue, 60611
(312) 440-1500, (800) 621-8311

Radisson Plaza Ambassador West
1300 N. State Parkway, 60610
(312) 787-7900, (800) 333-3333

Barclay Chicago Hotel
166 E. Superior, 60611
(312) 787-6000, (800) 621-8004

Best Western Inn of Chicago
162 E. Ohio Street, 60611
(312) 787-3100, (800) 848-2031

Blackstone Hotel
636 S. Michigan Boulevard, 60605
(312) 427-4300, (800) 622-6330

Chicago Lake Shore Hotel
600 N. Lake Shore Drive, 60611
(312) 787-4700, (800) 343-8908

Days Inn Congress Hotel of Chicago
520 S. Michigan Avenue, 60605
(312) 427-3800, (800) 635-1666

Drake Hotel Chicago
140 E. Walton Street, 60611
(312) 787-2200, (800) 445-8667

Essex Inn
800 S. Michigan Avenue, 60605
(312) 939-2800, (800) 621-6909

Fairmont Hotel
200 N. Columbus Drive, 60601
(312) 565-8000, (800) 527-4727

Four Seasons Chicago
120 E. Delaware Place, 60611
(312) 280-8800, (800) 332-3442

Hilton and Towers Chicago
720 S. Michigan Avenue, 60605
(312) 922-4400, (800) 445-8667

Holiday Inn Mart Plaza
350 N. Orleans Street, 60654
(312) 836-5000, (800) 238-8000

Hyatt Park Chicago
800 N. Michigan Avenue, 60611
(312) 280-2222, (800) 223-1234

Indian Lakes Resort
250 W. Schick Road
Bloomingdale, 60108
(708) 529-0200, (800) 334-3417

Inter-Continental Hotel
505 N. Michigan Avenue, 60611
(312) 944-4100, (800) 628-2468

Knickerbocker Chicago
163 Walton Place, 60611
(312) 751-8100, (800) 621-8140

Mayfair Regent
181 E. Lake Shore Drive, 60611
(312) 787-8500, (800) 545-4000

McCormick Center Hotel
Lake Shore Drive and 23rd Street,
60616
(312) 791-1900, (800) 621-6909

Midland Hotel
172 W. Adams Street, 60603
(312) 332-1200, (800) 621-2360

Morton Hotel
500 S. Dearborn Street, 60605
(312) 663-3200, (800) 843-6678

Oak Brook Hills Hotel and Resort
3500 Midwest Road
Oak Brook, 60522
(708) 850-5555, (808) 445-3315

Ritz Carlton
160 E. Pearson Street, 60611
(312) 266-1000, (800) 268-6282

Sheraton Plaza
160 E. Huron Street, 60611
(312) 787-2900, (800) 325-3535

INDIANA

Indianapolis

Adams Mark Hotel
2544 Executive Drive, 46214
(317) 248-2481, (800) 444-2326

Courtyard by Marriott
501 W. Washington Street, 45204
(317) 635-4443

Embassy Suites
110 W. Washington Street, 45204
(317) 236-1800, (800) 888-0071

Hilton at the Circle
Ohio and Meridian Streets, 46206
(317) 635-2000, (800) 445-8667

Holiday Inn Crowne Plaza
123 W. Louisiana Street, 45206
(317) 631-2221, (800) 465-4329

Hyatt Regency Indianapolis
One S. Capitol Avenue, 45204
(317) 632-1234, (800) 228-9000

**University Place Conference
Center and Hotel**
850 W. Michigan Street, 45202
(317) 269-9000, (800) 627-2700

Westin Indianapolis
50 S. Capitol Avenue, 46204
(317) 262-8100, (800) 228-3000

LOUISIANA

New Orleans

Bourbon Orleans Hotel
717 Orleans Street, 70116
(504) 523-2222, (800) 521-5338

Clarion Hotel New Orleans
1500 Canal Street, 70112
(504) 522-4500, (800) 824-3359

Fairmont Hotel
University Place, 70140
(504) 529-7111, (800) 527-4727

Hilton Riverside New Orleans
Poydras at Mississippi River, 70140
(504) 561-0500, (800) 445-8667

Holiday Inn Crown Plaza
333 Poydras Street, 70130
(504) 525-9444, (800) 522-6963

Hyatt Regency New Orleans
500 Poydras Plaza, 70140-1012
(504) 561-1234, (800) 223-1234

Inter-Continental Hotel
444 St. Charles Avenue, 70130
(504) 525-5566

Le Pavillion
800 Poydras Street, 70140
(504) 581-3111, (800) 525-9095

Marriott New Orleans Hotel
555 Canal Street, 70140
(504) 581-1000, (800) 228-9290

Meridien New Orleans
614 Canal Street, 70130
(504) 523-3341, (800) 543-4300

Monteleone Hotel
214 Royal Street, 70140
(504) 523-3341, (800) 535-9595

Omni Royal Orleans Hotel
621 St. Louis Street, 70140
(504) 529-5333, (800) 843-6664

Pontchartrain Hotel
2031 St. Charles Avenue, 70140
(504) 524-0581, (800) 777-6193

Radisson Suite Hotel New Orleans
315 Julia Street, 70130
(504) 525-1993, (800) 333-3333

Sheraton New Orleans Hotel
500 Canal Street, 70130
(504) 525-2500, (800) 325-3535

Westin Canal Place Hotel
100 Iberville Street, 70130
(504) 553-5100

MARYLAND

Baltimore

Days Inn Inner Harbor
100 Hopkins Place, 21201
(301) 576-1000, (800) 325-2525

Harbor Court
550 Light Street, 21202
(410) 347-9714

Holiday Inn Inner Harbor
301 W. Lombard Street, 21201
(301) 685-3500, (800) 465-4329

Hyatt Regency Baltimore
300 Light Street, 31202
(301) 528-1234, (800) 228-9000

Marriott Inner Harbor Baltimore
Pratt and Eulaw Streets, 21201
(301) 962-0202, (800) 228-9290

Omni Inner Harbor Hotel
101 W. Fayette Street, 21201
(301) 752-1100, (800) 228-2121

Radisson Plaza Lord Baltimore Hotel
20 W. Baltimore Street, 21201
(301) 539-8400, (800) 333-3333

Sheraton Inner Harbor Hotel
300 S. Charles, 21201
(301) 962-8300, (800) 325-3535

Stouffer Harborplace Hotel
202 E. Pratt Street, 21202
(301) 547-1200, (800) 468-3571

Tremont Plaza Hotel
222 St. Paul Place, 21202
(301) 727-2222, (800) 638-6266

MASSACHUSETTS

Boston

Boston Harbor Hotel
70 Rowes Wharf, 02110
(617) 439-7000, (800) 752-7077

Boston Park Plaza Hotel and Towers
50 Park Plaza, 02117
(617) 426-3323, (800) 966-7926

Colonnade Hotel
120 Huntington Avenue, 02116
(617) 424-7000

Copley Plaza Hotel
138 St. James Avenue, 02116
(617) 267-5300, (800) 776-6546

**Fifty Seven Park Plaza Hotel
Howard Johnson**
200 Stuart Street, 02116
(617) 482-1800, (800) 654-2000

Guest Quarters Suites Hotel
400 Soldiers Field Road, 02134
(617) 783-0090, (800) 424-2900

Hilton Back Bay
40 Dalton Street, 02115
(617) 236-1100, (800) 424-2900

Holiday Inn Goverment Center
5 Blossom Street, 02114
(617) 742-7630, (800) 874-0663

Lenox Hotel
710 Boylston Street, 02116
(617) 536-5300, (800) 621-9200

Marriott Copley Place
110 Huntington Avenue, 02116
(617) 236-5800, (800) 228-9290

Meridien Hotel Boston
250 Franklin Street, 02110
(617) 451-1900, (800) 543-4300

Omni Parker House
60 School Street, 02108-4198
(617) 227-6600, (800) 843-6664

Quality Inn Downtown Boston
275 Tremont Street, 02116-5694
(617) 426-1400, (800) 228-5151

Ritz-Carlton Hotel
15 Arlington Street, 02117
(617) 536-5700, (800) 241-3333

Sheraton Hotel and Towers Boston
39 Dalton Street, 02199
(617) 236-2000, (800) 325-3535

Weston Hotel Copley Place
10 Huntington Avenue, 02116
(617) 252-9600, (800) 228-3000

Cambridge

Charles Hotel at Harvard Square
One Bennett at Eliot Street, 02138
(617) 864-1200, (800) 882-1818

Hyatt Regency Cambridge
575 Memorial Drive, 02139
(617) 492-1234, (800) 233-1234

Marriott Boston Cambridge Hotel
2 Cambridge Center, 02142
(617) 494-6600, (800) 228-9290

Sonesta Royal Hotel
5 Cambridge Parkway, 02141
(617) 491-3600, (800) 343-7170

MICHIGAN

Detroit

Omni International Hotel Detroit
333 E. Jefferson Avenue, 48226
(313) 222-7700, (800) 843-6664

Radisson Pontchartrain Hotel
2 Washington Boulevard, 48226
(313) 965-0200, (800) 333-3333

Westin Hotel
Renaissance Center, 48243
(313) 568-8000, (800) 228-3000

MINNESOTA

Minneapolis

Crown Sterling Suites
425 S. 7th Street, 55415
(612) 333-3111, (800) 433-4600

Holiday Inn Minneapolis Downtown
1313 Nicollet Mall, 55403
(612) 332-0371

Hyatt Regency Minneapolis
1300 Nicollet Mall, 55403
(612) 370-1234, (800) 228-9000

Marquette Hotel
710 Marquette Avenue, 55402
(612) 332-2351, (800) HILTONS

Marriott City Center
30 S. Seventh Street, 55402
(612) 349-4000, (800) 228-9290

Omni Northstar Hotel
618 Second Avenue S., 55402
(612) 338-2288

Radisson Plaza Hotel Minneapolis
35 S. 7th Street, 55402
(612) 339-4900, (800) 333-3333

**Ramada Plaza Hotel
Minneapolis West**
12201 Ridgedale Drive, 55305
(612) 593-0000, (800) 2-RAMADA

Sheraton Park Place Hotel
5555 Wayzata Boulevard, 55416
(612) 542-8600, (800) 325-3535

NEW JERSEY

Morristown

**The Governor Morris Hotel
and Conference Center**
2 Whippany Road, 07960
(201) 529-7300

Headquarters Plaza Hotel
3 Headquarters Plaza, 07960
(201) 898-9100, (800) 225-1942

Newark

**Hamilton Park Executive
Conference Center**
175 Park Avenue
Florham Park, 07932
(201) 377-2424

Parsippany

Hilton Parsippany
1 Hilton Court
Route 10 and 287, 07054
(201) 267-7373, (800) HILTONS

Sheraton Tara Hotel
199 Smith Road, 07054
(201) 515-2000, (800) 525-3535

Princeton

Hyatt Regency Princeton
102 Carnegie Center, 08540
(609) 987-1234, (800) 233-1234

**Scanticon Princeton
Conference Center**
100 College Road E., 08540
(609) 452-7800, (800) 222-1131

Secaucus

**Holiday Inn/Harmon
Meadow Sportsplex**
300 Plaza Drive, 07094
(201) 348-2000

Sheraton Meadowlands Hotel
Sheraton Plaza Drive
E. Rutherford, 07073
(201) 896-9696, (800) 325-3535

NEW YORK

New York City

Park Inn Hotel
440 W. 57th Street, 10019
(212) 581-8100, (800) 231-0405

Doral Park Avenue Hotel
70 Park Avenue, 10016
(212) 687-7050, (800) 847-4135

Essex House
160 Central Park S., 10019
(212) 247-0300, (800) 228-9290

Helmsley Park Lane Hotel
36 Central Park S., 10019
(212) 888-1624, (800) 221-4982

Hilton and Towers New York
1335 Avenue of the Americas, 10019
(212) 586-7000, (800) HILTONS

Loews New York
569 Lexington Avenue, 10022
(212) 751-7000, (800) 223-0888

Holiday Inn Crowne Plaza
Broadway and 49th Streets, 10019
(212) 977-4000, (800) HOLIDAY

**Macklowe Hotel
and Conference Center**
141 W. 44th Street, 10036
(212) 869-5800, (800) 622-5569

Marriott Marquis New York
1535 Broadway, 10035-4017
(212) 398-1900, (800) 228-9290

Meridien Parker Hotel
118 W. 57th Street, 10019
(212) 245-5000, (800) 543-4300

Novotel New York
225 W. 52nd Street, 10019-5804
(212) 315-0100, (800) 221-3185

Pierre Hotel
2 E. 61st Street, 10021-8402
(212) 838-8000, (800) 228-3000

Plaza Hotel
Fifth Avenue and 59th Street, 10019
(212) 759-3000, (800) 228-3000

Regency Hotel
540 Park Avenue, 10021
(212) 759-4100, (800) 223-0888

Radisson Empire Hotel
44 W. 63rd Street, 10023
(212) 373-4550, (800) 333-3333

St. Moritz on Central Park
50 Central Park S., 10019
(212) 755-5800, (800) 221-4774

**Sheraton New York Hotel
and Towers**
811 7th Avenue at 53rd Street, 10019
(212) 581-1000, (800) 325-3535

The St. Regis
2 E. 55th Street, 10022
(212) 753-4500, (800) 334-8484

UN Plaza–ParkHyatt
One United Nations Plaza, 10017
(212) 758-1234, (800) 233-1234

The Waldorf Astoria/Waldorf Towers
301 Park Avenue, 10022
(212) 355-3000, (800) HILTONS

The Warwick Hotel
65 W. 54th Street, 10019
(212) 247-2700, (800) 223-4099

Wetbury Hotel
15 E. 69th Street, 10021
(212) 535-2000, (800) 321-1569

OHIO

Cincinnati

Clarion Hotel Cincinnati
141 W. 6th Street, 45202
(513) 352-2100, (800) 876-2100

**Drawbridge Inn
and Convention Center**
I-75 at Buttermilk Place
Ft. Mitchell, 41017
(606) 341-2800, (800) 354-9793

Hilton Cincinnati Terrace
15 W. 6th Street, 45202
(513) 381-4000, (800) 445-8667

Holiday Inn Eastgate
4501 Eastgate Boulevard, 45245
(513) 752-4000, (800) 465-4329

Howard Johnson Plaza Hotel
11440 Chester Place, 45246
(513) 771-3400, (800) 654-2000

Marriott Cincinnati
11320 Chester Road, 45246
(513) 772-1720, (800) 228-9290

Omni Netherland Plaza
36 W. Fifth Street, 45202
(513) 421-9100, (800) THE-OMNI

The Westin Hotel
Fountain Square, 45202
(513) 621-7000, (800) 228-3000

Columbus

Hilton Inn Columbus North
7007 N. High Street
Worthington, 43085
(614) 436-0700, (800) HILTONS

Holiday Inn Center Center
175 E. Town Street, 43215
(614) 221-3281, (800) 465-4329

Hyatt On Capitol Square
75 E. State Street, 43215
(614) 228-1234, (800) 233-1234

Radisson Hotel Columbus North
4900 Sinclair Road, 43229
(614) 863-0300, (800) 333-3333

Ramada University Hotel and Conference Center
3110 Olentangy River Road, 43202
(614) 267-7461, (800) 282-3626

Sheraton Inn Columbus
2124 S. Hamilton Road, 43232
(614) 861-7220, (800) 866-9067

OREGON

Portland

Benson Hotel
SW Broadway at Oak, 97205
(503) 228-2000, (800) 426-0670

Hilton Portland
921 SW 6th Avenue, 97204
(503) 226-1611, (800) HILTONS

Holiday Inn Portland Airport Hotel
8439 NE Columbia Boulevard, 97220
(503) 256-5000, (800) HOLIDAY

Marriott Hotel Portland
1401 SW Front Avenue, 97201
(503) 226-7600, (800) 228-9290

Red Lion Inn Janzen Beach
909 N. Hayden Island Drive, 97217
(503) 283-4466, (800) 547-8010

Sheraton Portland Airport Hotel
8235 NE Airport Way, 97220
(503) 281-2500, (800) 325-3535

PENNSYLVANIA

Philadelphia

Adam's Mark Hotel Philadelphia
City Avenue and Monument Road, 19131
(215) 581-5000, (800) 444-2326

The Barclay
237 S. 18th Street, 19103
(215) 545-0300, (800) 421-6662

Four Seasons Hotel
One Logan Square, 19103
(215) 963-1500

Holiday Inn Independence Mall
Fourth and Arch Streets, 19106
(215) 923-8660, (800) HOLIDAY

Latham Hotel
135 S. 17th Street, 19103
(215) 563-7474, (800) 528-4261

Penn Tower Hotel
34th and Civic Center Boulevard, 19104
(215) 387-8333 (800) 356-PENN

Philadelphia Marriott West
111 Crawford Avenue, 19428
(215) 941-5600, (800) 228-9290

Radisson All Suites Hotel
18th Street and The Parkway, 19103
(215) 963-2222, (800) 325-3535

Sheraton University City
36th and Chestnut Streets, 19104
(215) 242-9100, (800) 325-3535

TENNESSEE

Nashville

Doubletree Hotel
315 4th Avenue N., 37219
(615) 244-8200, (800) 528-0444

The Hermitage Hotel
231 6th Avenue N., 37219
(615) 256-0739, (800) 251-1908

Holiday Inn Crowne Plaza
623 Union Street, 37219
(615) 259-2000, (800) HOLIDAY

Loews Vanderbilt Plaza Hotel
2100 West End Avenue, 37203
(615) 320-1700, (800) 23-LOEWS

Marriott Nashville Hotel
One Marriott Drive, 37210
(615) 889-9300, (800) 228-9290

Opryland Hotel
2800 Opryland Drive, 37214
(615) 871-5824

Sheraton Music City Hotel
777 McGavock Pike, 37214
(615) 885-2200, (800) 325-3535

Stouffer Nashville Hotel
611 Commerce Street, 37203
(615) 255-8400, (800) HOTELS-1

TEXAS

Dallas

Adolphus Hotel
1321 Commerce, 75202
(214) 742-8200, (800) 331-4812

Bristol Suites
7800 Alpha Road, 75240
(214) 233-7600, (800) 922-9222

Double Tree Hotel at Lincoln Centre
5410 LBJ Freeway, 75240
(214) 934-8400, (800) 222-TREE

Fairmont Hotel
1717 N. Akard Street, 75201
(214) 720-2020, (800) 527-4727

Grand Kempinski Hotel Dallas
15201 Dallas N. Parkway, 75248
(214) 789-3031, (800) 426-3135

Holiday Inn Downtown
1015 Elm Street, 75202
(214) 748-9941, (800) 465-4329

Hyatt Regency Dallas
300 Reunion Boulevard, 75207
(214) 651-1234, (800) 233-1234

Loews Anatole Hotel
2201 Stemmons Freeway, 75207
(214) 748-1200, (800) 223-0888

Marriott Quorum
14901 Dallas Parkway, 75240
(214) 661-2800, (800) 228-9290

Plaza of the Americas Hotel
650 N. Pearl Boulevard, 75201
(214) 979-9000, (800) 225-5843

Southland Center Hotel
400 N. Olive Street, 75201
(214) 922-8000, (800) 272-8007

**Stouffer Hotel Dallas
Market Center**
2222 Stemmons Freeway, 75207
(214) 631-2222, (800) 325-3535

Westin Hotel Galleria
13340 Dallas Parkway, 75240
(214) 934-9494, (800) 228-3000

Houston

Days Inn Downtown
801 Calhoun Street, 77002
(713) 978-7400, (800) 444-2326

Doubletree Hotel
2001 Post Oak Boulevard, 70056
(713) 961-9300, (800) 528-0444

Embassy Suites Southwest
9090 SW Freeway, 77074
(713) 995-0123, (800) 553-3417

Four Seasons Houston
1300 Lamar Street, 77010
(713) 650-1300, (800) 332-3442

Holiday Inn Crowne Plaza
2222 W. Loop S., 77027
(713) 961-7272, (800) 327-6213

**Houstonian Hotel
and Conference Center**
111 N. Post Oak Lane, 77024
(713) 680-2626, (800) 456-6338

Hyatt Regency Houston
1200 Louisiana, 77002
(713) 654-1234, (800) 233-1234

Omni Houston
4 Riverway, 77056
(713) 871-8171, (800) 843-6664

Ritz-Carlton Houston
1919 Briar Oaks Lane, 77027
(713) 749-7600, (800) 241-3333

**Sheraton Crown Hotel
and Conference Center**
15700 JFK Boulevard, 77032
(713) 442-5100, (800) 325-3535

Sofitel Hotel
425 N. Sam Houston Parkway E.,
77060
(713) 445-9000, (800) 231-4612

**The Woodlands Executive
Conference Center and Resort**
2301 N. Millbend Drive
Woodlands, 77380
(713) 367-1100, (800) 533-3052

WASHINGTON

Seattle

Four Seasons Olympic Hotel
411 University Street, 98101
(206) 621-1700, (800) 223-7662

Hilton Seattle
6th and University, 98101
(206) 624-0500, (800) 426-0535

Holiday Inn Crowne Plaza
1113 6th Avenue, 98101
(206) 464-1980

Sheraton Hotel and Towers Seattle
1400 6th Avenue, 98101
(206) 621-9000, (800) 325-3535

Stouffer Madison Hotel
515 Madison Street, 98104
(206) 583-0300, (800) 468-3571

Warwick Hotel
401 Lenora, 98121
(206) 443-4300, (800) 426-9280

Westin Hotel Seattle
1900 5th Avenue, 98101
(206) 728-1000, (800) 228-3000

WISCONSIN

Milwaukee

Grand Milwaukee Hotel
4747 S. Howell Avenue, 53207
(414) 481-8000, (800) 558-3862

Hyatt Regency Milwaukee
333 W. Kilbourn Avenue, 53203
(414) 276-1234, (800) 223-1234

Marc Plaza Hotel
509 W. Wisconsin Avenue, 53203
(414) 271-7250, (800) 558-7708

Wyndham Milwaukee Center
139 E. Kilbourn Avenue, 53202
(414) 276-8686, (800) 822-4200

Index

A

A/B split testing method, 98–100
Act, Contact Software International, 144
Advertisements, using to fill seminars, 102–8
Advertising, resources, 103, 106
Advertising agencies, 92
Advertising medium, choosing the best, 102
Adweek, 92
All-in-One Directory, 110
American Business Lists, 96
American Seminar Leaders Association (ASLA), 16, 52, 70–71, 170
American Society of Association Executives, 148
American Thermoplastic Company, 58
Artline Industries, 60
AT&T, 85
Audiovisuals
    choosing and using, 61–71
    putting the audio into, 67–68

B

Bacon's Publicity Checker, 110
Bacon's Publishing Company, 110
Banquet style seating, 158–59
BeaverPrints, 79
Better Photos and Custom Lab, Inc., 116
Bill Good Marketing, 52
The Bill Good Marketing System, 144
Bios, 115
Bookmasters, 60
Bound workbooks, 57–58

BPI Media Services, 110
Bradley Communications Corp., 118
Brainstorming techniques; *see* Branching
Branching, 41–43
Brilliant Image, 66
Brochures, 85
The Business Institute, 4

C

Church and religious organizations, 149
Cinegraph Communications, Inc., 66
CIS Marketing, Inc., 101
Classroom style seating, 154–56
Client list, 140–41
Colad Inc., 59
Columbia Books, Inc., 147
Company brochures, 117, 140
Confirmation letters, 32
Confirmation phone calls, 33
Consultant, hiring, 51–52
Contacts, 10
Copywriters, 91–92
The Copywriters Handbook (Bly), 82
Corporate market, tapping, 135–44
Cover letters, 114, 139–40
Crane Duplicating Service, Inc., 60
Creative Vinyl Products, 59

D

Dale Carnegie and Associates, Inc., 170
Dearborn Publishing Group, Inc., 52
Dinner & Klein, 60

Direct mail
   checklist and timeline, 101
   promoting your seminar, 94–101
   resources, 78–79, 100
   testing, 98–100
   three primary formats, 78
Direct-mail approaches, three most
      successful, 85–90
Direct Mail List Rates and Data, 95
Direct mail promotion, cost of,
      100–101
Direct Marketing Association
      (DMA), 94
DVC Industries, 59

E

"Educainment," mastering, 165–67
Emerald Publishing, 52
Encyclopedia of Associations, 147
Endorsements, 140–41
The Executive Speechwriter Newsletter,
      167

F

Financial seminars; *see also* National
      Association of Securities Dealers
      (NASD)
   designing, 39–47
   success of, 17–19
Financial Visions, 53
Flipcharts, 63
Folder Factory, 60
Folders, 58
Follow-up, 141–42
Fraternal Organizations, 148–49

G

Gale Research Company, 147
Garrett Financial Group, 53
Gavel, 75
Gebbie Press, Inc., 110
Graphic Artist Guild, 91
Graphic designers, 91

H

Handout materials, 54–60
   assembling, 57–58
   creativity, 55–57
   importance of, 54–55
   resources, 58–60
High-touch selling, 3
Hot copy
   resources, 82
   writing, 79–82
*How to Make Advertising Twice as
      Effective at Half the Cost* (Lewis),
      106
How to Write a Good Advertisement
      (Schawab), 106

I

Ibbotson Associates, 53
Idea Art, 79
Ideal Photo, 116
In-house seminar
   advantage of, 145–46
   marketing strategy, 149–50

J

Joint venture seminars, 10–11

K

Karasik's law of sales, 35

L

Leads, organizing, 143–44
Letter invitations, 88
Letter of agreement, sample of, 146

M

The Magic Wand Technique, 25
Mailing lists
   choosing the right, 95
   components of, 96–97

Mailing lists—*Cont.*
  getting the best, 97–98
  where to purchase, 95–96
Marker boards, 63–64
Marketing machine, creating, 128
Marketing Masters, Inc., 53
Marketing material, 29
  designing, 82–84
  producing, 78–93
  resources, 82–84
Mastermind group, assembling, 39–40
Material design, using a professional,
  90–92
MCI Telecommunications, 85
Media, using, 166
Media coverage
  resources, 110
  steps to getting, 109–12
Media kits, components of, 112–18
Mehrabian, Professor Albert, 161–64
Microphones, four styles of, 68–69
Microphones and sound systems
  guidelines for using, 69–70
  resources, 70–71
Mighty Mouse method, for free
  seminar promotion, 119–20
Minnesota, University of, 61
Mitchell Davis, 118
Modular design approach (MDA), 41
Modules, prioritizing, 43–44
Money, 104
Monstad and Christensen, 53
Motivation
  law of, 21
  ultimate law of, 22

N

National Association of Securities
  Dealers (NASD); *see also* Financial
  seminars
  getting approval from, 46–47
National Speakers Association, 170
*National Trade and Professional
  Associations of America*, 147
National Underwriters Company, 66

Nervousness, conquering, 171–75
Newspaper ads, creating successful,
  103–5
No-shows, reducing, 127–28

O

Objectives, understanding, 17–19
Overhead projectors, 63

P

Paper Direct, 59
People
  disturbing, 22
  understanding, 21–22
Phone-mail-phone, 149
  strategy of, 136–38
Photographs, 116
Photo printing, resources, 116
Prepackaged seminars
  advantages of, 48–49
  customizing, 51
  disadvantages of, 49–50
  resources, 52–53
Prerecorded sound, 70
Presentation formats, 9–10
Presentation skills, essential elements
  of, 161–64
Presentation style, best, 164
Presenter, primary objective, 165
Press agent, becoming your own, 109
Press releases, 112–13
Previous appearances, list of, 116–17
Printer, finding the best, 92–94
Professional associations, 147–48
Promotional materials
  checklist, 82–85
  presenting, 139–41
Psychological advantages, focusing
  on, 19–21
Publicity, turning into profits, 119
Public relations, resources, 118
Public relations firms, 92
Public Relations Society of America,
  118

Q

Queblo, 59
Question and answer sessions,
   handling, 168
Quotes and poems, 166–67

R

Radio Contacts, 110
Radio-TV Interview Report, 118
Registration contract, 30–32
Registrations, increasing with free
   publicity, 109–20
Registration table, 160
Reliance Plastics, 59
Response Call, Inc., 108

S

Sale closing, 29–38
   building relationships, 33–34
   closing techniques, 35–37
   complimentary consultations, 38
   initiating the relationship, 29–33
Sales objection, eliminating, 3
Sample question lists, 117
Selye, Dr. Hans, 171
Seminar brochures, 117, 140
Seminar invitations, wedding style, 89
Seminar leaders, secrets of the
   greatest, 161–70
Seminar Leaders University, 16
Seminar leading, performing well,
   168–70
Seminar market, in-house, 145–50
Seminar marketing, using the
   telephone, 121–28
Seminar materials, 141
Seminar modules, identifying, 41–43
Seminar participant evaluation, 36
Seminar participants, dealing with,
   175–79
Seminar registration, resources, 108
Seminar room
   arranging for success, 151–60
   lighting, 152

Seminar room—*Cont.*
   seating, 152–59
   temperature, 151–52
Seminars, 9, 11–16, 72–77
   best months and days, 72–73
   best time of the day, 73
   checking your calendar, 72
   choosing the site, 74–75
   the confirmation letter, 76–77
   delivery skills, 15–16
   designing your own, 50
   design skills, 15
   focusing on, 40
   minimizing meeting room
      expenses, 76
   prepackaged versus customized,
      48–53
   providing choice, 73–74
   public, 11–12
   resources of, 16, 75–77
   secret ingredient of, 39, 45–46
   selling skills, 16
   seven techniques of, 44–45
   sources of humor, 167
   sponsored, 12–14
Seminar selling
   approach, 4
   attendance of, 2
   definition of, 1
   golden rule, 20
   strategy of, 2, 4–5
   and your time, 2–3
Seminars Plus; *see* CIS Marketing, Inc.
Service clubs, 148–49
Slide projectors, 62
Smart Money, 104
SourceBook, 75
Speakers bureaus, getting booked
   by, 150
Speeches, 10
Sprint, 85
Standard Rates and Data, 95, 103
Stories, telling, 165–66
Stress Without Distress (Selye), 171
Success, prerequisite for, 14–16
Successful Money Management, 53
Sutton, Willie, 144

T

TADA, 23–28, 49, 50, 51, 58, 62, 82, 84, 90, 95, 96, 111, 115, 150; *see also* Target audience
choosing, 24–26
the magic marketing strategy, 135–36
suggested, 26–28
survey, 25–26
Talk shows, method for getting on, 118
Target audience, 39; *see also* TADA
focusing on, 79
Target Audience Design Approach; *see* TADA
Target Marketing, 100
Tearsheets, 116–17
Telemagic, Inc., 143
Telemarketers, hiring of, 122–23
Telemarketing
expected results, 123–24
timing, 126
Telemarketing script, 124–26
Telephone marketing
advantages and disadvantages, 121–22
golden rule, 123–24
Telephone registration script, 30–32
Television Contacts, 110
Ten question quiz, 36–37
Tested Advertising Methods (Caples), 106
Theater style seating, 156–58
Three-ring binder, 57
Toastmasters International, 170
Tracking sheets, 126
Trade and professional associations, 147–48
Triangle Printing, 59
Turn, Touch, Talk technique, 67

U

University of Southern California, 161–64
Unseminar
definition of, 129–30
guidelines for, 132–33
prerequisite for, 130
promoting, 131
rewards of, 133–34
why the format works, 130–32
USA 800, 108
U-shaped style seating, 158–59

V

Verbal delivery, 161, 163–64
Vinylweld, 59
Visual aids
choosing the best, 62–64
guidelines for using, 64–65
resources, 65–66
use of, 61–62
Visual delivery, 161–63
Visual Horizons, 66
Vocal delivery, 161, 163

W

The Wharton School of Business, 61
What's in it for me (WII-FM), 21, 30, 34–35
Who's Who in Association Management, 148
Words That Sell (Bayan), 82
Workshops, 10
Worth, 104

Y

The Yearbook of Experts, Authorities, and Spokeperson, 118

Other books of interest to you from Irwin Professional Publishing . . .

BOGLE ON MUTUAL FUNDS

New Perspectives for the Intelligent Investor

John C. Bogle

Explains the basic principles of mutual fund investing and reveals the unique nuances and subtleties of this alluring field.
1-55623-860-6   320 pages

STOCKS FOR THE LONG RUN

A Guide to Selecting Markets for Long-Term Growth

Jeremy J. Siegel

Offers solid strategies for long-term investment success, showing investors how to understand and interpret the movements of the market over time.
1-55623-804-5   250 pages

THE MONEY MONARCHS

The Secrets of Today's 10 Best Investment Managers

Douglas J. Donnelly

Examines profiles of the top 10 U.S. money managers according to performance, volatility, investment requirements, and investment philosophy.
1-55623-898-3   250 pages

TAKING CONTROL OF YOUR FINANCIAL FUTURE

Making Smart Investment Decisions with Stocks and Mutual Funds

Thomas E. O'Hara and Helen J. McLane

Offers a unique selection of stock picking techniques from the National Association of Investors Corporation Stock Selection Guide, which is used successfully by thousands of investors and investment clubs,
0-7863-0139-2   250 pages

About the Author

Paul Karasik is president of The Business Institute, an organization dedicated to providing the financial industry with development in sales, marketing, and management skills.

He is the author of three business classics, *Sweet Persuasion* and *Sweet Persuasion for Managers,* published by Simon & Schuster and *How to Make It Big in the Seminar Business,* published by McGraw-Hill. In addition, his column, "Seminar Selling" appears monthly in *National Underwriters* magazine.

Paul is the founder and president of the American Seminar Leaders Association.

Products and services offered by The Business Institute include:

- On-site seminar selling and sales training programs
- Keynote presentations
- Sales motivation
- Audio and video learning programs
- Consulting services
- Turn-key financial services

For more information on how The Business Institute can help you and your organization achieve more professional success please call or write:

The Business Institute
899 Boulevard East, Suite 4H
Weehawken, NJ 07087
201-864-9149